Fornes

THEATER: Theory/Text/Performance

Enoch Brater, Series Editor
University of Michigan

Fornes

Theater in the Present Tense

Diane Lynn Moroff

Ann Arbor

THE UNIVERSITY OF MICHIGAN PRESS

1999   1998   1997   1996   4   3   2   1

*A CIP catalog record for this book is available
from the British Library.*

Library of Congress Cataloging-in-Publication Data

Moroff, Diane Lynn.
    Fornes : theater in the present tense / Diane Lynn Moroff.
       p.   cm.
    Includes bibliographical references and index.
    ISBN 0-472-10726-7
    1. Fornes, Maria Irene—Criticism and interpretation.   2. Fornes,
Maria Irene—Dramatic production.   3. Fornes, Maria Irene—
Chronology.   4. Theater—United States—Production and direction—
History—20th century.   5. Feminism and theater—United States—
History—20th century.   6. Women in the theater—United States—
History—20th century.   I. Title.
PS3556.O7344Z77   1996
812'.54—dc20   96-10153
                                                              CIP

To Libby Moroff and Saul Moroff
for teaching me to read

Acknowledgments

I would like to thank my friends, particularly Karen Perlman, Barbara Burch, Craig Kramer, and Margaret Moroff—but all of them, really—for inspiring enough self-confidence to enable me to see this project through.

Particular thanks also are due to Enoch Brater, who has served as my mentor, both for this project, which began as my dissertation under his direction, and, more generally, for my intellectual growth. Helene Keyssar's criticisms of this manuscript have been momentous in the manuscript's evolution. I thank LeAnn Fields for her persistent kindness and encouragement. I also thank William Brightman for his invaluable editorial suggestions.

Contents

Introduction

Maria Irene Fornes has been writing, directing, and producing award-winning plays for over three decades now, though she has received far less attention from the press and academia than she deserves. That attention is increasing—she is being studied and taught with increasing fervor—but her emphasis on spectacle, on the interplay of imagery both literarily and literally evoked and of characters' confrontations with that imagery, has made her work less penetrable than those of her more pedantic and famous contemporaries such as Sam Shepard, David Mamet, and Marsha Norman. As a remedy, this book will explore Fornes's poetic and lyrical drama, heeding, particularly, her drama's self-consciousness about the relationships between its various spectacular parts, from a gun perched in a stage corner to spaces between bodies and words to Fornes's painstaking architectural constructs.

The scholarship around Fornes's theater tends to be highly theoretical, composed for an audience of converted academics—which lends to, rather than diminishes, her marginalization in theatrical and academic worlds alike. While critics have successfully invoked the semiotic complexities of Fornes's theater, they have done so without making her texts accessible to a broader constituency. I offer here, as a necessary supplement, careful readings of Fornes's plays structured by descriptive accounts of those moments and attributes that make Fornes's drama lyrical: the emphasis on the sensual over the intellectual experience of her characters and the patterns, direct and digressing, of characters' encounters with the especially animated spectacle of Fornes's theatrical environments. These visual and poetic configurations on Fornes's stages are at the crux of that meaning created by the simultaneous texts of what the spectator sees and what the spectator hears.

The image in Fornes's theater ultimately takes precedence over the text, a trait sometimes ignored by her otherwise astute and reverent critics. Fornes makes lyrical poetry out of bodies and props, framing narrative scenes within scenes often silent, or accompanied by music alone, wherein thought and emotion are worked out and conveyed through the image itself. In *Sarita,* for example, the protagonist suffers the punishment of madness and estrangement for her adulterous affair with Julio, though that affair is then both validated and celebrated by Fornes's interruption of the drama with the romantic and perceptibly seductive image of Sarita and Julio poised in lovemaking beneath the legs of a kitchen table. Or, in *Mud,* though Henry and Lloyd prove more powerful than Mae, a scene in which Mae forces Lloyd's head back, prying open his mouth to force pills down his throat, contradicts that narrative with the image of her power. And in *The Conduct of Life* Nena is a particularly vulnerable victim, a child continually raped by an army lieutenant who tortures political prisoners, and yet the image at the play's center of her peaceably shelling peas with another woman at a kitchen table reverberates with the calm, strength, and compassion that save her by the play's end. Fornes is adept at evading her audience's expectations, punctuating and in turn metamorphosing her plays' politics with theatrical spectacle, with what we see—as, paradigmatically, in the final scene of *Fefu and Her Friends,* in which Fefu has been exonerated by the text for Julia's murder but is still left holding the smoking gun.

Fornes, as woman and playwright—and, indeed, like so many of her idiosyncratic characters—is unconventional and irreverent. She willfully makes use of anything available to her, from realistic to absurdist conventions, from Aristotelian to Brechtian techniques. Her approach is often shamelessly erratic, which means that she makes use of distancing devices when they are convenient, while she may reject them for an unself-conscious assumption of narrative authority in the next scene; she will emphasize music for one act's purposes then deprive her audience of a single additional note. The demands of her "messages" dictate her form as whimsically as their unruly structures would indicate.

One consequence of her eclectic approach to form has been the goading of her textual analysts. Moments such as the climactic encounter of *Fefu and Her Friends,* in which the play's generally representational structure is exploded for the sake of withholding closure, have compelled debates not only about the theatrical instance's meaning but about formal characterization of the plays. While the search for rubrics has been revealing for critics in the particular, it has also led to contradiction and occasional abstruse theorizing. I locate Fornes as a lyrical, poetic playwright within the structural contradictions just cited; her simultaneous reverence and irreverence for theatrical methodology result in the beguiling incongruity of a kind of visible melody, a synchronized cacophony.

Samuel Beckett's plays, the quintessential lyrical dramas of the twentieth century, are her most obvious antecedents. Like Beckett, Fornes subjects her characters to the theater that only in part represents the world beyond the theater. In her three decades of writing, the politics of both her form and content have become more sophisticated but always within a context of deliberately articulated semiotics in which her primary concern has been the power dynamics between characters explored meticulously through the characters' physicality. As *Waiting for Godot's* Vladimir and Estragon's drama is demarcated by their relationships to each other, to the tree and road, to their shoes and bowlers, Fornes's characters' stories are manipulated within similar dramatic worlds, visually memorable for their evocative constructions—the befouled foundation of *Mud;* the series of boxes wherein *Sarita's* drama takes place; the multileveled set of *Conduct,* in which a character's gestures circumscribe identity: Nena shelling peas, Fefu fixing her plumbing. The progress-less stories of Beckett's theater also echo in Fornes's theater. Her plays are rarely plot driven; more often, structure is the consequence of characters represented by their participation in small and frequently absurd scenes whose juxtapositions equal dramatic events. Fornes's characters talk, pose, and posture incessantly, and Fornes's theater lends significance to those "small" acts with scrupulous theatrical framing; characters and audience alike are continually subjected to the carefully crafted and manipulated extraliterary spectacle of the body, light, music, color, and space.

For so many modern and contemporary theater practitioners, precisely because of the text's expansion to multidimensioned spectacle, the theater is a third space, hovering between the fictive and the real, with elements of each inherent to it, and of direct relevance to both, to art and to the art of living. In this vein Fornes works with the theater as did the most prominent twentieth-century lyrical playwrights before her. Her early dramas recall Jean Cocteau's in their absurdist imagery teetering on the edge of symbolism; the inexplicable but utterly significant props on the stage of *Tango Palace*—"a guitar, a whip, a toy parrot, a Persian helmet, two swords, a cape, a compass, a muleta, a pair of bull-horns, six banderillas, two masks in the form of beetles' faces" and "the shrine . . . decorated with a string of flower-shaped lightbulbs" (70)—suggest a dramatic world like Cocteau's equally cluttered *Wedding on the Eiffel Tower,* wherein characters' identities are determined in part by the objects they encounter. Her increasing emphasis on the gravity of role-playing, the character as determined by his or her context, and the slipperiness of language resurrect Jean Genet's *The Maids* and Eugène Ionesco's *Rhinoceros.* And lugubrious atmospheres conjure the dramas of the Irish lyrical playwrights William Butler Yeats and Lady Gregory.

Fornes's is frequently absurdist theater, like Beckett's, though more conservative both formally and philosophically.[1] Her early work was contemporaneous with the alternative theater of the 1960s—the experimental theater of Jerzy Grotowski in Poland and the Living Theatre of Julian Beck and Judith Malina in New York—though, again, her plays were neither the "poor" theater of Grotowski's Laboratory Theatre nor the improvised and spontaneous happenings that grew out of Beck's and Malina's "guerrilla theater" but, rather, narratively tamed, less frictional, and theatrically controlled versions of each. Not as cerebral perhaps as Edward Albee or Tom Stoppard, in the United States and England Fornes was playing similar games with absurdist logic within plotless narratives. With all these writers Fornes shares the lyricism resulting from the interplay of spectacle with texts ultimately focused on the ominous and modern condition of human vulnerability.

As has been true to various degrees for most of Fornes's critics, it is her theatricality—or, in W. B. Worthen's term, "the 'enunciators' of the stage" (1989, 168)—and its political implications that I find most compelling. Paradoxically, it is Fornes's keen attention to and manipulation of the spectator's sensory experience through spectacle that has, as noted, both distinguished her and contributed to her deficient fame. Whereas a Mamet play supports a relatively painless literary glossing, Fornes's plays tend to resist literary analysis, as in *Fefu,* in which women continually infiltrate the stage space, shifting the spectator's focus and upsetting the narrative flow. That quality has made her plays of special interest to contemporary theatrical critics, who find in Fornes's dramas particularly ripe territory for the exploration of subjectivity represented through an actual human body—a topic of distinct importance to feminist critics, who often contest even the possibility of a genuine female subject given the historical facts of patriarchal control over language and representation. Worthen, for example, finds that *Fefu* highlights the position of the female subject on the stage, usually objectified, by "dramatizing the audience's implication in the conduct of the spectacle . . . [and] exploring the ideology of stage gender through a sophisticated use of stage space to construct a 'dramatic' relation between stage and audience" (175), a conclusion that reverberates with Jill Dolan's in her seminal text *The Feminist Spectator as Critic* (1988). Dolan suggests that Fornes's best work is consistent with "the materialist critical project . . . to denaturalize the psychological identification processes implicit in representation. When the representational apparatus is foregrounded, its once mystified ideology becomes clear" (14). Fornes's *Sarita* and *The Conduct of Life* particularly illustrate this phenomenon for Dolan, who argues that Fornes, like Brecht, rejects realism that "naturalizes social relations imposed by dominant ideology and mystifies its own authorship" (106). By foregrounding the image over the word, Fornes compels her spectators not to accept as truth but "to question the interactions and relationships played out in the representational space" (106).

For Helene Keyssar and Deborah R. Geis, through the staging of polyphony and the Brechtian *gestic* monologue, respectively, Fornes has provided a stage that actively resists patriarchal representation of the female subject. Keyssar notes Fornes's "rejection of monologism and the patriarchical authority of the drama in performance. [Fornes and others of her "genre" attempt] to create a dramatic discourse that celebrates rather than annihilates or exiles difference" (1991, 93). Keyssar, too, is attentive to Fornes's simultaneous visual and literary texts and their capacity to represent otherwise marginalized subjects. "The spectacle and dialogue of theatre mediate," she writes of Fornes's and others', "but do not resolve differences; the essential strategy of these plays is to bring together diverse discourses in such a way that they interanimate each other and avoid an overarching authorial point of view" (95). Similarly, Deborah R. Geis delineates Fornes's success at the representation of women on her stage as "subject[s]-in-process or . . . nonunified subject[s]" (1990, 292). Most recently, Stanton B. Garner Jr. has included Fornes's plays in his study of those contemporary women's plays that attempt "a recuperation of the embodied female subject, a return of corporeality to the creative interaction of the subject and its environment" (1994, 188).

In her 1984 essay, "The Real Life of Maria Irene Fornes," Bonnie Marranca offers this characterization:

> What Fornes, as writer and director of her work, has done is to strip away the self-conscious objectivity, narrative weight, and behaviorism of the genre to concentrate on the unique subjectivity of characters for whom talking is gestural, a way of being. There is no attempt to tell the whole story of a life, only to distill its essence. Fornes brings a much needed intimacy to drama and her economy of approach suggests another vision of theatricality, more stylized for its lack of exhibitionism. In this new theatricality, presence, that is, the act of being, is of greatest importance. The theatrical idea of presence is linked to the idea of *social being* expressed by character. . . . This realism is quotational, theatre in close-up, freeze frame. (29, 31)

As Marranca's comments submit, Fornes's success has been in the spectacleization of the entire theatrical event. All meaning in her theater comes from the act and consequences of looking for both characters and spectators. It is never enough to hear text alone: Fefu's announcement "I like being like a man" must be weighed against a stage populated only by women, where Fefu and the rest of us will see only women, a stage on which "Man" can only be an abstraction.

Fornes's "theatre in close-up" demands that looking take priority over any other act, as has been true in her own career. Fornes's attention to what can be made visible in the theater, and why that matters, ensues logically from the career steps that led to her playwriting. Born in Havana, Cuba, in 1930, Fornes came to the United States in 1945 and worked as a textile designer from 1957 to 1960. She left New York from 1954 to 1957 to paint in Paris and then rejoined New York's avant-garde art scene just before the explosive 1960s, when she immediately became a fixture in the off-Broadway theater. She was a founding member and president of New York Theatre Strategy from 1973 to 1978, and she taught for the Theatre for the New City in 1972 and 1973, at the Padua Hills Festival from 1978 until the present, and at International Arts Relations (INTAR) from 1981 until the present. A member of the Dramatists Guild, American Society of Conductors, Authors, and Publishers (ASCAP), League of Professional Theatre Women, and the Society of Stage Directors and Choreographers, Fornes won her first Obie Award for Distinguished Playwriting in 1965 for *Promenade* and *The Successful Life of 3,* and she has won seven more since, both for playwriting and for playwriting and directing. She has been the recipient of numerous grants and fellowships, from such prestigious sources as the Rockefeller Foundation, the National Endowment for the Arts, and Yale University.

Though Fornes says she sees no connection between her onetime career as a painter and that of a playwright and director, her description of her response to Roger Blin's 1954 production of *Waiting for Godot* is strikingly visual. She saw the play in French, of which she spoke not a word, and had never read the play in English. "But," she told Scott Cummings in an interview, "what was happening in front of me had a profound impact without even understanding a word. Imagine a writer whose theatricality is so amazing and so important that you could see a play of his, not understand a word, and be shook up" (52). The "theatricality" Fornes refers to here obviously has had a critical impact on her own work. In a private correspondence from Herbert Blau to the associate director of the Rockefeller Foundation, concerning Fornes's then titled *There! You Died!* (later titled *Tango Palace*), Blau wrote:

> If you can imagine a rather exotic Latin development of the sort of experience we've come to know through Beckett, that's it. The play has a very devilish charm and wry, dark humor. One feels in it both a disarming sense of play and a good deal of well observed behavior.

Blau's astute adjectives might also characterize Fornes's response to questions from critics, responses that often further complicate rather than clarify the critics' tasks. When asked to comment on topics ranging from whether her

work is realistic to her feminist goals, she is as often evasive as downright disrespectful of contemporary critical preoccupations. Pressed by Scott Cummings
to define theatrical realism, Fornes insisted that realism in *her* theater will not
come from minutiae of detail or photo-accurate reproductive sets but from the
actors, from the players. She elaborates:

> Realism is just behavior. I like acting that is true, that I can see and believe
> something is happening to that character. You [the actor] have to be well
> grounded, grounded not with your intellect but with your humanity, your
> body, your carnality. (54)

Stanton B. Garner Jr. refers to this formal characterization as realism "in terms
of [the] physiological base" of the subject's "corporeality" (192). Reality is
finally grounded in the body in Fornes's theater. Fornes relies less on narrated
themes than on the truth the body tells. Fornes's early theater events, remarkably irreverent of certain theatrical traditions (the plays start anywhere, are full
of nonsense and contradiction, end where they began) are often more like series
of truthful moments placed incidentally side by side, real to the actors, real in
their presents. Fornes shrugs off those critics who complain about incoherence
in her dramas. She has not been trying to be coherent, she implies; she has been
trying to be honest. And honesty can elude narrative coherency.

She has been frankly anti-intellectual in her musings on the process of
playwriting, insisting of *Promenade,* for example, in an interview with Richard
Shepard in the *New York Times* in 1965: "The play comes very deeply from my
own consciousness. I didn't sit down and figure out who were to be the characters. The explanation is an afterthought; there are images I believe in completely." Other comments offer context for this bow to inspiration by asserting
her respect for the theater over the text. "Playwriting has less to do with language than novel writing does," she told Shepard. "It's language in a very special way. Language is like the motor that starts a machine. How the machine
performs, what dynamics it creates—that's what counts." Almost three decades
later, in a special section of the *Performing Arts Journal* (1994) devoted to the
avant-garde, Fornes describes the creative process in strikingly similar terms.
She told Bonnie Marranca: "I believe that there's a creative system inside of us.
It's a system that's almost physical. I can compare it with the digestive system or
the respiratory system. . . . The writing is not asking me for permission but it is
taking force and just going" (22).

Her method of playwriting is ultimately visual; she is building rather than
writing a text, which is why my readings of her later plays attempt to move

methodically and thoroughly from image to image, scene to scene. To build rather than write a play necessitates a more multifaceted engagement for the playwright. When Fornes discusses her own development as playwright, director, and even as an actor of sorts, what is most striking is the sense that for her these roles are inseparable, part and parcel of her own theatricality. For *Fefu and Her Friends* Fornes removed the fourth wall of realist theater not only by inviting the spectator's physical intrusion into the production but by submitting to the beckoning of the theatrical space she saw offstage as well. In "I write these messages that come" (1977) Fornes describes the process of developing the space for the production of *Fefu*. She found parts of her stage in the practical space of the theater: the dressing room, the business office, and so on. The discovery of this space began to control the shaping of the drama: "It was the rooms themselves," Fornes insists, "that modified the scene. . . . [The scenes] were written [the way they were] because the space was there" (36–37). In 1964 Fornes remarked to Beverly Byers Pevitts: "A playwright has to have a very abstract mind and has to see a play like an architect. One has to see the whole building and also structure and foundations and how these things are made and see it so it doesn't fall apart" (317).

In this holistic vein Fornes stubbornly defends her romantic—sensual rather than intellectual—lyricism, the implicit and explicit subject of certain disparaging criticism of her work. She asks Cummings:

> Have you even been with a person when just being with them makes you see everything in a different light. A glass of beer has an amber, a yellow that you've never seen before. . . . It *is* more beautiful. It isn't that you want it to be more beautiful.

Fornes partially means to elude her political critics and their categories. Those characters that make troublesome decisions—to abandon a child, to cheat on a spouse—are forgiven. They are only guilty of responding "to the beauty that's around [them, and] there's no deception in that," she insists (Cummings 1985, 55).

The feminist issues relevant to Fornes's characters' most provocative deeds have spurred a round of debates among critics. As Fornes's plays resist formal and generic classification, they also resist political classification—as does Fornes herself. The debate about whether or not Fornes is a feminist playwright has primarily centered around the types of women she has characterized in her theater. In "Irene Fornes: The Elements of Style" (1986) Ross Wetzsteon concludes that feminist criticism has been, for Fornes, an "approach that too often turns her plays into pronouncements." Fornes commented to Wetzsteon: "Party members don't think I'm much of a feminist. The only bad review *Fefu* got was in *Ms.* magazine—the reviewer thought I was portraying women as whining victims. I don't know how to respond when people think in party lines" (45). In her essay "Creative Danger" (1985) Fornes elaborates:

> If I think of it, it seems natural that I would write with a woman's perspective, but I am not aware that I am doing any such thing. I don't sit down to write to make a point *about* women. . . . Often, there are misunderstandings about my work because it is expected that as a woman I must be putting women in traditional or untraditional roles, or roles of subservience or subjugation or dominance, to illustrate those themes. . . . To understand *Mud* as being about Mae's oppression and . . . *The Conduct of Life* about the subjugation of Latin American women is to limit the perception of those plays to a singleminded perspective. (13)

While not dismissing those themes, Fornes reminds her audience to avoid reading theater as we do literary texts. The theater, when it makes the most constructive use of its own form, cannot support "singleminded" perspectives; it is the product of too many players (writer, director, actor, set designer), the site for too many voices. As Helene Keyssar has articulated, Fornes's theater is polyvocal; by definition, then, it sustains multiple perspectives, determined by the constant flux of voices and presence.

While Fornes has provided many rich and complex voices for different women characters, her own has remained unpretentious and even a little ingenuous. The consequences have been occasional estrangement. As late as 1991, Fornes nearly found herself ostracized by her own. At the Second Annual Women Playwrights "Voices of Authority" conference, according to Rachel B. Shteir in *American Theatre* (1991), amid a discussion about political correctness and the playwright, "Maria Irene Fornes went so far as to call for the evasive humanist 'standard of excellence' as a way to judge work. When the audience booed, Fornes retaliated by shouting, 'My work is as political as anybody's!'" (54). Of course, Fornes's plays are as political as anyone else's, and it is part of the critic's task to analyze those politics. Though Fornes and I may disagree on certain terminology, I consider both her plays and my readings of them feminist, particularly insofar as we both seek to explore the representation and construction of gender and insofar as Fornes is especially attentive to women's social, economic, and political experience.

In the end Fornes is delightfully inconsistent and, as such, keeps the classifiers at bay. No one can accuse Fornes of a single-minded perspective; hers has been as divided for thirty years as her characters' have been in the hour or two of their stage lives. From Fornes's first produced work, *Tango Palace,* performed in 1963 at the Actors Workshop in San Francisco, a vaudevillian pas de deux between two outrageously eccentric characters, to her most recently published work, *What of the Night?* in *Women on the Verge* (1993), a disturbing drama concerned with sexualized abuses of power, her extraordinary range of topics and form have also prevented her critics from being single-minded; read together, their texts passionately contradict themselves and one another, testimony to Fornes's diversity and philosophical irreverence.

Before the 1980s, when she began to highlight the issues of violence and abuse, imaging those trespasses more and more overtly, Fornes's early plays were received by New York drama critics with a kind of joy—as was Fornes herself. Her presence alone inspired significant commentary. In 1966, in the *Village Voice,* Stephanie Harrington described Fornes as a woman who "could use four-letter words at a tea party . . . without ever being accused of not being a lady. She is unassuming, little—cute, even, though she probably wouldn't react well to the word. Or maybe she'd like it. She's not predictable" (1). Harrington quotes an old friend of Fornes's: "[Fornes is] Alice and the Red Queen: utter innocent and the complete sophisticated worldling. She's the totally untutored who can solve problems in calculus without knowing what calculus is. She knows everything, but outside the verbal framework of other people." Fornes emerges as an eccentric who says of herself: "I don't read. But I talk a lot" (33).

In the 1960s her critics were routinely exhilarated by all that talking. In an August 1966 *New York Post* article, "Rebellion in the Arts," Jerry Tallmer remarked that "there were those who thought *Promenade*—an opera-farce of practically everything—the best and funniest work in its season, off-off-Broadway or wherever." In April 1969 Robert Pasolli announced in his article "'You take a yes & a no'" in the *Village Voice,* where he thinks the spectator's gratification comes from:

> Fornes's minimal art says certainly not all, but something and something with implications for more. This is why her theatrical moments are delightful. Delight in her plays is simply the sensation of surprise that what seemed like nothing does, in fact, amount to something, sometimes to a great deal. (57)

Pasolli particularly responds to Fornes's characters, "lunatics" like Dr. Kheal of the play by that name and ignoramuses like He, She, and 3 of *The Successful Life of 3.* He admires "a specialty of her characters: an off-hand, flip attitude which is based on an outrageous and entirely natural ignorance of 'the facts.' One of the things which Miss Fornes knows about people is that reality is what's in their heads, not what's outside" (57). He, She, and 3 were especially popular off-Broadway for their humanness, their embracing of ignorance, as Fornes allowed them such dramatic activities as picking their teeth, yawning, and sleeping. Fornes's characters' irreverent and theatrical lives, the "life of vaudeville" and "insouciance" of the players in *Promenade,* add up, for Pasolli, to their being "infectious. The bright amorality of their lives makes them recognizable as our reflections" (58).

That empathic experience, when Fornes's dramas become less fun and more work, proves difficult for the critics; their responses become more troubled and their personal engagement more intense. With insight Al Carmines told Jerry Tallmer in August 1966, "She is not, or not yet, a social playwright, but she has that strand which could be developed—and she's just Brechtian enough" (24). From *Fefu* forward, whether appreciative or disparaging, reviews become both more political and impassioned. In the 14 January 1978 *New York Times* Richard Eder describes *Fefu* as "uneven but fascinating," and "the dramatic equivalent of a collection of poems":

> Each conversation, each brief scene tries to capture an aspect of a central, anguished vision. Some possess great strength, and a fine verbal and visual precision. In others, the intention is visible but not realized, whether because the writing falters or the performance does. . . . It is an imperfect evening, but there are moments of such splendor in it that it is like the imperfection of a friend.

Where Eder finds the spectators moving from room to room "engaging," and a "defect of self-consciousness . . . balanced by the usefulness of having one's mind move," Walter Kerr wrote in the *New York Times,* on 22 January 1978, that he stuck it out only in the hopes that he "*might* find a play in the very next room" and used the opportunity to leave the theater, avoiding the question-and-answer session following the performance. Ross Wetzsteon calls the play "a flawed but fascinating and frolicsome feminist farce," whose form itself makes "a provocative feminist argument" (1977, 36–37). Frank Rich's response to *The Danube* in the *New York Times,* on 13 March 1984, strikes a moral tone: "As a writer, Miss Fornes has a responsibility not just to parade serious issues across the stage, but to illuminate them. This she has failed to do." Mimi Kramer's review of *Uncle Vanya* is decidedly conflicted: "a beautifully acted, intensely absorbing production," "tremendously effective visually," and marred by "pointless" use of spectacle (e.g., in the Rossini framing the acts) and, more important, by the

interpretation, which Kramer found overly distorting of Chekhov's original
(*New Yorker,* 4 January 1988). And, while Ruis Woertendyke found *Abingdon
Square* thematically successful ("Ms. Fornes shows us the restrictions of our gender roles and dissolves the stereotypes that have so long littered our stages"), that
critic also notes that "the [fragmented] form of the play is not so successful as its
content . . . [making] it difficult to become more than intellectually involved in
Marion's story" (1988, 266); in contrast, Anthony Adler, in April 1990 in
Chicago magazine, remarks, "this [Brechtian] device fragments the narrative and
neutralizes the melodrama, making us less inclined to cry over it so we can get
a better look at what's going on underneath" (90).

It is the order of approach that trips up Fornes's critics. As I investigate
throughout this text, Fornes is not dramatizing a story as much as she is offering
her spectators the opportunity to discover a story—or a character or an idea—
within her theater. She inverts the traditional process and requires the critic to
invert his or her task in turn. Indeed, her descriptions of the development of her
playwriting philosophy are true to this inversion. When Fornes went to the
Actors Studio in the 1960s, she did so "with the interest of somebody who
wants to find out what is an actor" but from that experience developed a
method of characterization critical to her plays' aesthetics. Fornes describes this
process to Cummings:

> My writing changed when I first found out what the principle of [Strasberg's]
> Method is. My writing became organic. I stopped being manipulative. . . . [In
> *The Successful Life of 3*] what one character says to another comes completely
> out of his own impulse and so does the other character's reply. The other
> character's reply never comes from some sort of premeditation on my part or
> even the part of the character. The characters have no mind. They are sim-
> ply doing what Strasberg always called "moment to moment." There I was
> applying the Method technique for the actor to my writing and it was bring-
> ing something very interesting to my writing. (52)

The technique of Fornes's writing workshops in the mid-1980s moved
from yoga to a process she calls "visualization," which Fornes helped to guide.
She would ask her students, for example, to remember something from childhood connected with water then to visualize the place then to draw the place,
to "let somebody come into that place. . . . Watch the person for awhile and see
what they do. . . . You are completely passive. You begin to distinguish the difference between when you're manipulating and when you're not" (54). She
would then guide a little further by pushing the visualization into fiction with a

line of dialogue or piece of a situation. Cummings succinctly describes the progression: "So the last thing to come is language or speech." Fornes, pleased with this summary, responds, "Yes. . . . I don't know why words want to become authoritarian" (55). Experience takes precedence over the language of experience. Much of the irreverence of Fornes's dialogue and musical interludes (the 1960s plays are full of song and dance, which often ironically enhance their sometimes more serious purposes) results from this aesthetic. She trusts the experience of the actors/characters to justify the entire work of art.

Visual priorities notwithstanding, Fornes's reverence for the power of the word is acute. She makes a critical distinction between the actor and the character in relation to language:

> What I want language to be is an expression of the characters, but a very careful expression so that they or the words don't get carried away and become their own expression. . . . I want to catch the process of the forming of thought into words. (Cummings 1985, 55)

With this assertion Fornes moves beyond her faith in poetic inspiration to a more complex explication of the artist's role. That moment—"the process of the forming of thought into words"—is critical to Fornes's work. The language of her plays becomes entirely and appropriately relevant; the tendency toward language patterns that resemble non sequitur, or even nonsense, finds its source here: she is articulating, and sometimes imaging, the *process* of the thought, so the thought, the idea, the expression, would be false if it were expressed already eloquent, already whole. Ultimately, this is a moral concern for Fornes; to respect the process of thought is to respect the process of developing philosophy and to undermine facile conclusions.

Fornes's theatrical productions repeatedly assert language's status as dependent cog to the theater's wheel. As a woman playwright, the ambition to underscore that relationship may stem from a nagging sense that she is using someone else's words; as a lyrical playwright—a visual poet even—Fornes is responding to a more general sense of the gaps between our verbal articulations of reality and what is happening at any given moment. Fornes has been explicit about her desire to make her theater "real" in both these contexts: she means to disclose a certain reality of women's experience as well as the more trustworthy, even if unspeakable, subtext of language.

The power of Fornes's spectacle and the fragility of language notwithstanding, Fornes uses words with considerable authority and insight. In the end words have actual, tangible effect; Fornes depicts such strong relationships between characters and their utterances that her characters seem virtually to hold their words in their hands. They are in awe of their own language. The women in Fornes's dramas, often denied other tools for survival, treat words like hammers and nails, trying desperately to make language work for them. In her most solemn dramas the female protagonists approach language from as many directions as they can. Fefu and her friends talk ceaselessly about the moments they are in as well as more generally about their experiences of the past and the futures they are trying to enter and create. *Mud*'s Mae carries a textbook with her as if it were a Bible, hoping that even the book's formal descriptions of sea life will help her to locate her true self. In search of ever elusive control, Sarita writes letter after letter to her lover and mumbles to God, even though neither appear to be listening. And the women of *The Conduct of Life* spin out monologues as if they were physical structures that might protect them from the forces of a larger drama.

Highly charged dramatic moments emerge in Fornes's plays in a manner that recall Desdemona's prattle just before Othello comes to kill her or Ophelia's "mad" speech before the Queen. The words are not precisely sensible; some spectators will hear only nonsense. But others may feel that they are hearing the character's—or the woman's—own words for the first and only time. There is another kind of lyricism in these essential moments in Fornes's drama, thematic and emotionally laden. As for Shakespeare's women characters, these moments are often terrible, the moment just before death or madness, a moment of complete estrangement from others, estrangement from context, but they are *owned* moments, fully realized by the women within them. The play's narrative briefly dissolves away from the image of a woman alone with her words.

Thematically—and perhaps incongruously, given her irreverence toward realism as a form—Fornes's persistent representation of women places her within a tradition of American social dramas about women's lives as shaped by society and culture, a tradition marked by such playwrights as Rachel Crothers, Susan Glaspell, and Lillian Hellman. As is often true in those dramas as well, there is frequently an element of sadness and angst, particularly for the women in Fornes's plays, but coincident with that angst is Fornes's intoxicating delight at the theater's transformative capacities. In all of Fornes's plays the theater is replete with metaphorical implications for the audience's larger theaters as well as having its own ominous and powerful life.

With an eye toward what men and, particularly, women do and say on Fornes's stages, I focus in this book on four of Fornes's full-length plays, *Fefu and Her Friends* (1977), *Mud* (1983), *Sarita* (1984), and *The Conduct of Life* (1985), and her most recently published play, *What of the Night?* (1993); each chapter explores different aspects of the coinciding issues of theatrical form and theme laid out here. *Fefu and Her Friends,* for example, represents a world perched between real life and the theater wherein women theatricalize themselves as a way of testing their own "characters." In my reading of *Mud,* I consider Mae's struggles for self-determination through language and the theatrical world's, both her own and the spectator's, tenacious obstacles to that struggle. In *Sarita* I locate the combined powers of art and politics as one of Fornes's primary concerns and the use an artist can make of those forces. And *The Conduct of Life* I read as an explicit summons to women spectators to recognize the means to assert authority through the theater, either as actors or as spectators. The concept of the palimpsestic sexualization of character is at the center of the fifth chapter, which reexplores the plays of the first four chapters and *What of the Night?.* Fornes's plays of the 1960s and early 1970s—the pre-*Fefu* plays—for which I provide brief précis in the following chapter, chart the course for the exploration of these issues in her later plays.

Ross Wetzsteon (1986) tells an anecdote about the mutual inspiration and admiration of friends Susan Sontag and Maria Irene Fornes. One night in 1960 Fornes insisted that the two forgo a party in the East Village and go home to their West End apartment to write, an evening that evidently sparked careers for both women. In her essay "Against Interpretation" (1964) Sontag claims, "[in] place of a hermeneutics we need an erotics of art." She continues:

> The aim of all commentary on art now should be to make works of art—and, by analogy, our own experience—more, rather than less, real to us. The function of criticism should be to show *how it is what it is,* even *that it is what it is,* rather than to show *what it means.* (14)

That is largely what I try to do here, in the context of exploring what Fornes's plays can illuminate about themselves, about theatrical metaphor and theatrical power in our real lives. I hope to illustrate how these plays can enhance both the professional and amateur student of the theater's thinking about the nature of the image in the theater, the interplay of theatrical elements—actor and prop, actor and set, actor and stage, actor and actor, spectator and theatrical event—and about certain parallel dynamics in human relationships between women and between women and men.

Theatrical Presents

Maria Irene Fornes's early works, each a notable departure from its predecessor and all written within a remarkably short span of five years, include *Tango Palace* (1963), *Promenade* (1965), *The Successful Life of 3* (1965), *A Vietnamese Wedding* (1967), *Molly's Dream* (1968), and *Dr. Kheal* (1968). In this last, Dr. Kheal trumpets his knowledge of "the poetry of space in a box"— what, in essence, Fornes "writes" with her imagist theater: lyrical presentations, lyrical via language and spectacle alike, of dramatic events; from poetic monologues and sharply imbalanced repartee; to He, She, and 3's chorus, "let me be wrong, but, Oh, not to know it," to Handel; to rooms suddenly smoke-filled and stages suspended in air, a basement perched provocatively above a living room. Lyricism surfaces in the elaborate schema of characters' power plays, their emotional manipulations, and their responses to the barrage of wayward theatrical spectacle to which Fornes subjects them. Characters' narratives are produced by the theater, its props, its sets, its ambience.

A vaudevillian element characterizes most of these early plays, and a playfulness characterizes all of them. Each is irreverent, sometimes inconsistent, occasionally preachy, frequently silly. They each also have moments of exceptional theatrical sophistication, a keen awareness of their own contexts, limits, and reach. Each is at least in part about the theater itself, particularly about the way characters are characterized by those on the stage with them, by the stages and sets themselves, and by the audiences for which they perform. As this chapter will explore in detail, *Tango Palace* uses the paradigms of certain symbiotic roles in relationships, theatrical and otherwise, to show how roles are defined and controlled in antithesis to others' roles. *Promenade* suggests the possibility of transcending certain roles within a theatrical context; an audience, for example, someone to play to, can alter the nature of the play. *The Successful Life of 3* describes the pleasures, despite the trials, of theatrical lives. The play sets up formally what Fornes eventually explores more thematically (in *Dr. Kheal,* e.g.)— that is, the rewards of self-theatricalization. *A Vietnamese Wedding* and *Molly's Dream* explore the surprising distinctions between "character" and "role."

The spectator's identification and empathy with characters is at the core of Fornes's theatrical philosophy. Much of her commentary on these issues involves gender considerations, mostly because Fornes is responding to questions from critics and interviewers about the role of gender. In a special issue of the *Performing Arts Journal* (1983) devoted to women playwrights, Fornes offers a sideways glance at gender concerns with the assertion, "I have been thinking about the question of identifying with the opposite sex, not just observing the opposite sex but being one with it," though she then temporarily abandons any specific reference to gender and speaks more generally about the issue of identification, which, gendered or not, is ultimately political in its relationship to the rules that govern our social behavior. She explains that "it is through identification that we learn to become whole human beings. The experience of others becomes our own. And our experience endows details that we observe in the lives of others with a depth that benefits our understanding." We are, finally, very separate and distinct individuals, she asserts—that is, "we do not share a lifetime with any other person"—yet "we are one with the rest of humanity and that is not a choice. . . . We are one with the kind ones and the beautiful ones and the talented ones, but we are also one with the victims of crimes and with the murderers" (90). Fornes is beginning to detail her particularly social aesthetic. Both Fornes's playwriting and the subject of her plays often are precisely about sharing experience and enabling identification with an other.

The link between identification and gender relations lies for Fornes in compassion. "Compassion," she writes, "is of course a result of identification, and so is hatred." Fornes envisions humanity as utterly interconnected, transcendent, and so, she avers,

> my intention is not necessarily to promote kindness to the opposite sex but something ultimately more interesting, which is that any human being is a member of our species and if we do not allow our imagination to receive the experiences of others because they are of a different gender, we will shrivel and decay. (90)

The theater, she suggests, is a place in which to stage experience so that the spectator can "receive" that experience and achieve "identification." Her early

plays particularly suggest concentric rings of experience, from the character outward to the spectator. The theatrical context determines the dramatic character
and governs the poetic life of that character; spectators are asked to identify,
then to scrutinize, our own theatrical texts and the resulting parts we play.

The relationship between Isidore and Leopold in *Tango Palace* is paradigmatic of
the relationship between playwright or director and character, teacher and student, master and slave, lover and beloved—though Isidore, "an androgynous
clown," may be an ironic authority figure at best. The theatrical space is highlighted by an almost excessive use of theatrical prop, and its limits identified by
the "door . . . bolted with an oversize padlock," the presence of both actors on
the stage from the start, Leopold emerging from inside a canvas sack. The set
comes ostentatiously furnished with a Queen Anne walnut armchair, Louis
Quinze secretary, Louis Quatorze gilded mirror, a shrine with masks, a whip,
swords, and "a string of flower-shaped lightbulbs," among other items. The
characters themselves are decorated in unmistakable costumes, Leopold in a
business suit (in sharp contrast to the color and chaos surrounding him) and
Isidore in "a man's hat and pants, high-heeled shoes, and a silk blouse" with a
flower corsage (70).

Isidore gets to play both director and actor, much as he plays both man and
woman. After setting the scene—"Isidore makes a gesture and his shrine is lit.
He makes another gesture and chimes sound"—he opens the drama with,
"Look what the stork has brought me" (71). He then plays the role of chorus;
picking up his guitar, he announces, "Song and guitar accompaniment by
Isidore." When Leopold begins to explore the stage, Isidore narrates his
encounters for him: "Queen Anne walnut armchair. Representing the acme of
artistic craftsmanship of the Philadelphia school." Within moments he is directing Leopold, teaching him to dance by example (72). He literally holds the
script in his hands in a pack of cards he carries with him that appear to be directions for both characters' action and speech; throughout the play he flips a card
each time he "feels he has said something important" (70), the stage directions
indicate, and, really, each time he affects the action.

The cards give him a kind of omnipotence, and the props give him the
means to carry out his power when his disciple gets out of hand: when Leopold
reaches for the whip Isidore intercepts him: "This is my whip," Isidore says,
using it on Leopold, "And that is pain" (72). Leopold's first line, "I don't have
anything" (73), confirms his status. Later Isidore accuses him of being a parrot,

because Leopold imitates him. "Do you want to be a moron for the rest of your life? Always being pushed around?" he asks provocatively, given that he has allowed Leopold no other choice. Leopold is the actor whose any efforts at rebellion are thwarted. When he dares to set fire to one of Isidore's cards—that is, to try to manipulate the script—Isidore manipulates *him* into thinking that would have been a kind of suicide. The two argue about what would have happened had Leopold seen his rebellion through, until Isidore says, "Go on, burn them if you want," Leopold nervously refrains, and Isidore smugly remarks, "Wisdom" (77).

Finally, there is freedom for neither Leopold nor Isidore from this dramatic text, as Isidore's cards make inarguable: though his tossing them around the stage succeeds his articulations, the cards are those articulations scripted; despite his apparent authority, this character is not free to utter anything but the text that has been put into his hands. His eventual death confirms this. Even Leopold admits to that by affirming that his murdering of Isidore at the play's end was simply the response to direction: "The moment came," he says. "The only moment when it could be done. It possessed me and I let it take me" (88). The theater event eventually obliterates the director, although stage directions suggest that it also spurs the director into a new place. After the murder Leopold and Isidore soar to a spectacular heaven of harps and angels, "for the next stage of their battle" (88), one that appears interminable.

Leopold wants to believe in a world beyond the characters' theater. He insists that "there are moments when I've felt this is not all there is. . . . Close your eyes. . . . Imagine . . . that all is calm" (78). His desire makes him naive; both Isidore and the audience members know that no such place exists; nothing outside of the theater could be as remotely controlled and calm as what occurs within the theater, no matter how chaotic those events are. Art lends order even through the depiction of conflict. But Leopold's vision may be apt insofar as their theatrical space is part of a larger theatrical space.

The play offers the theatrical role as a metaphor for any interdependent role. Isidore taunts Leopold with the suggestion that his own death will be Leopold's freedom: "Gore me. That's the answer" (82), he says. To the extent that the playwright's death frees the character, or the master's death frees the slave, Isidore tells the truth. All roles require their inversions for definition; the lover needs a beloved to confirm his or her part. *Tango Palace* underscores the theatrical element to all human relationships, particularly abusive ones. While we agree to play parts, we are subordinate to the dramas that script those parts. When we accept our roles as they come to us, the world is a theater beyond our control.

Only a third party can alter the confines of this trap. Isidore describes this world to Leopold:

> We have only a vertical line. The space around us is infinite, enclosed as it may be, because there is not a third person. And if the space around us is infinite, so is, necessarily, the space between us. (76)

As long as these two characters continue to define each other, their roles are binding. But the audience can play the third point on Isidore's metaphysical map. The audience, or the world outside of *Tango Palace*'s theater, might be defined in antithesis to the theater and hence can suggest the possibility of a movement beyond the play's internal paradigmatic relationships. The audience can play the role of student to the theater's teacher, garner the theater's knowledge, and make something new of itself.

As in *Tango Palace,* in *Promenade* any character provides something against which another character can find definition. The rich are not the poor, the Servant is not the people she serves, the Mayor not the people he rules, and the Jailor not the Prisoners he pursues. Though the play's mantra recited by the Servant suggests that the game of role-playing is inherently transformative, the reverse appears to be true within this drama. Accompanied by the Prisoners, named 105 and 106, the Servant sings:

> Be one and all
> Be each and all.
> Transvest,
> Impersonate,
> 'Cause costumes
> Change the course
> of life.

> (24)

Yet, although nearly every character in the play trades a costume for another, none of their dramatic fates is altered in turn. The rich women undress and redress; the Prisoners exchange their jail clothes for the Soldier's jackets; Miss Cake, by wrapping a stole around her shoulders, rises in rank to become the Mayor's mistress—but the rich are rich at the drama's end, and the Servant wanders off, lonely and poor.

That definitive stagnation notwithstanding, in the theatrical present every character undergoes a transformation. Throughout their romantic, orgiastic games, characters ricochet all over the stage, in and out of one anothers' arms, and in and out of their expected, socially determined behavioral patterns. This world has different expectations of its players than does the surrounding "real" world. As a rule, the characters games are sweet and sexy, the rich people's marked by innocuous flirtations, the Jailor and Prisoners politely speaking French to each other even while the Jailor attempts to trap them: *"Après vous . . . . Pas du tout. . . . Je vous en prie. . . . Mon plaisir. . . . Permettez-moi"* (19), they sing.

The Servant speaks the play's giddy moral:

> We've come to one conclusion
> That's readily discerned:
> A lot of satisfaction
> Does away with discontent.
>
> (20)

The characters provide one another with a theatrical present in which they can pursue pleasure unabashedly (strip naked, picnic in the grass, make love), and in particularly theatrical ways—that is, by changing costumes and putting on shows in the form of the rich women's striptease, for example, or the Prisoners' ubiquitous slapstick. They provide one another with enough of an audience to justify their theatricality. At least as long as they have an audience, Fornes suggests, anything is possible; roles may be entirely transformed.

When the crowd dissipates and the characters lose their audience, the drama comes to its sad close: the Servant ambles offstage to consider her loneliness, and the Mother of the Prisoners mourns the sadness of the text in which she is enmeshed:

> There are many poor people in the world
> Whether you like it or not
>
> . . . .
>
> When I go, no one will water my plants
>
> . . . .
>
> Good night.
>
> (44–45)

The jealousies and inconsistencies that Fornes illustrates throughout the drama—the romantic musical chairs of the rich people's diversions, the manipulative games the Mayor plays with his audience—are the stuff of danger and pain off the stage but of music and dance on the stage. As Beckett's Vladimir and Estragon do at certain moments, *Promenade*'s characters find fun and humor in the theatrical world to which they are bound but not freedom from that world. The dismal note on which the play ends reminds the spectator that role-playing alone will shatter little in the way of context, although in our larger theaters we might imitate the rebellions of these players, make up different theatrical games, and at the very least find different roles to play.

As were the characters from *Promenade,* those of *The Successful Life of 3* are rewarded for their simple virtues of spiritedness in role-playing. Their stories— their dramas in general—are merely vehicles for the game of role-playing. Fornes ensures that the spectator will understand that the characters of this drama—He, She, and 3—are little more than impersonators through their names and what amount to masks: on cue throughout the drama She "thinks with a stupid expression," He "looks disdainful," and 3 "looks with intense curiosity" (48).

Fornes provides these characters with a three-way marriage; by scene 3 ten years have already passed, and the three sit on their porch, dozing, peeling potatoes, and sewing. It is a perfect marriage, however ridiculous it may sometimes seem. In their own mean and selfish ways these characters could not be more accommodating. They make excellent use of one another, enabling every whim. 3 needs He to hold the popcorn because, as he says, "I can't feel her up and eat at the same time if I hold the bag" (53); He holds the popcorn. She wants some economic support, so she marries He, choosing him arbitrarily over 3. He's career as a store detective is dependent on his having someone to arrest; 3 indulges him by becoming a criminal. Any role a character chooses to adopt is met, sometimes with derision or ridicule, surely, but met nonetheless by the other characters in their marriage.

He, She, and 3 constitute the quintessential theatrical family in their adaptability to theatrical form. Insofar as character is subservient to drama—that is, determined by the drama—these characters do whatever the text tells them to do. Though He and She are officially married, 3 is She's most consistent sexual partner, probably even the father of her children; He apparently gets no "action," and, though he complains considerably, he does nothing to change the course of these predetermined events. When She insists she is tired of this story and leaves He and 3, the men simply wait patiently on the porch for her inevitable return.

Fornes does not judge these characters for their obedience. To the contrary, she seems as fond of them as they are of one another, a fondness only barely affected by everyone's mutual contempt for the passivity that prevents them from ever overcoming their script. Like the characters in *Promenade,* He, She, and 3 make the most of their theatrical world, turning their tragedies into spectacle, into song and dance, just as Fornes has turned their characterizations into spectacle by way of their masks.

The entire theatrical event of *The Successful Life of 3* is a tribute to ignorance and impotence, as their finale zealously indicates:

> Let me be wrong.
> But also not know it.
> Be wrong,
> Be wrong,
> And, oh, not to know it.
> Oh! Let me be wrong.

(65)

Their ignorance enables happy role-playing. Virtually void of any moralizing, the play is pure celebration of even the most pathetic imaging of human needs. Because their ignorance allows them to believe there is no world beyond their world, allows them to exist only for one another's sake, He, She, and 3's actions have no consequences. They are endowed with the theatrical gifts of an audience—in us and in one another—and the right to make a spectacle out of whatever they choose.

When the audience is again explicitly acknowledged, when theatrical role-playing will necessarily reverberate in the audience's experience, the theatrical games become a bit more complex. In *A Vietnamese Wedding,* a theatrical experiment rather than a play according to Fornes, the playwright explores the formal aspect of character, its formulation by the context provided by the playwright, the actors, and the audience, both theatrically and culturally. The text was designed for participation in a Vietnam War awareness event (in 1967) and, as such, seeks to humanize the "other." Four scripted readers enact the event with audience participants, who actually fill the seats marked for Matchmaker, Groom, Father, and so on (118). Though the context will likely be alien and unfamiliar to Western audiences, when they adopt the roles the context prescribes, they inevitably transform the context into something habitable and familiar.

The drama, insofar as there is one, is determined by the readers' recounting of a Vietnamese myth, the story of two brothers, Tan and Sung, and Tan's unnamed wife, "as fair as a white lotus and as fresh as a spring rose" (123). Their triangular relationship, like He, She, and 3's before them, is mutually dependent, their fates to their deaths fully entwined. Fornes suggests that their tragedy symbolizes "conjugal and fraternal love" (124) and thus tells an old and familiar story.

Fornes embellishes that familiar story by describing Vietnamese marriage as a process of choosing spouses in terms of economic convenience, according to social standing, education, and moral history, which effectively—particularly in thematic terms—puts the idea of character into quotes. Though the myth of Tan, Sung, and the maiden provides a context for the ceremony, it is *only* context; character will be determined in this event by the participants who fill the context. Fornes literalizes the formative significance of both the spectators' and the actors' input to the theatrical event. Meaning will be wholly dependent on the manner and aura of the participants and their interactions; role, therefore, is stripped of any inherent qualities, underscored as a formal construct alone.

Molly's Dream also seeks to distinguish between character and role. At the drama's start, despite the title's implications that Molly has the responsibility of a narrator or playwright, larger theatrical forces seem to conspire against her. Fornes moves her audience quickly through narrative layers, eventually suggesting a movement as far as possible from literary narrative to theater: the play opens with Molly reading the story of another waitress in another saloon then interrupts that story with the appearance of a young man in the doorway whose presence triggers Molly's dream. The drama shifts from Molly's "real life" to the fiction she reads then to an almost pure theater of dreams—less her dreams than the young man's or, even, the playwright's.

Each character plays a role partially stereotypical to the genre of romance. Mack plays the macho bartender tyrannizing both his employee and his clientele, Molly plays the lonely and love-starved waitress, and Jim (whom the young man becomes in Molly's dream) plays the sexy stranger. Jim best typifies Fornes's play with role and character in this drama. For his completion his character requires his Hanging Women, literally a group of women who hang off of him, physically and imagistically defining him as a sexual being. With the Hanging Women he comes to represent sexuality more generally—or, at least, male sexuality in its most theatrical sense—and, through her initial response to him, Molly comes to represent female sexuality, or female sexuality as it can be defined in relation to male sexuality in *its* most theatrical sense. The Hanging Women put Molly and Jim's love story in its appropriately facile context. True love, they claim, is "one very long, / Very narrow, / Very old idea" (111). For a while, until a new character disrupts the predictable, all the characters will play their roles exactly according to the expectations of that script.

Alberta, a deceptively secondary character (a woman who wanders into the bar dressed as Shirley Temple), both embraces the genre of romance in its most conventional trappings and makes something more profound and honest of the form. When she lets her hair down to engage with John, another man in

the bar, in "vampirical love-making poses," she looks "sensuous and glam-
orous" (111); that is, she plays flawlessly certain predictable aspects of a woman's
role in romance. But she also sings a song that pays tribute to the quintessence
of romance:

> You have brought me to my senses
> You have made sense of me
> And the sense of me is you.
> I hear. I see. I smell. I taste. I touch.
> Oh, love.
> My life is senseless without you.

> (113)

By insisting that romance gives life to human sexuality and sensuality, Alberta
redeems the genre. It may be Alberta's inspiration that enables Molly to avoid
the temptations of the theatrical dream scripted for her; that is, she does not
become one of Jim's Hanging Women. Alberta has suggested that honest sexuality can overcome the form, any form, even while it comfortably inhabits
aspects of certain structures. The conventional form of romance is not itself at
fault for the limitations of certain roles prescribed by the form; rather, it is the
limitations of those inhabiting the form that limit, in turn, the roles we might
play.

The struggle for dominance between the drama and the character continues in *Dr. Kheal,* as the eponymous protagonist, alone on the stage throughout,
tries to assert his character over the drama, particularly through the relationship
he establishes with his audience. Though originally Dr. Kheal would like to
think he is entirely independent of his audience—and therefore speaks comfortably in a monologue—the fact that he does not soliloquize can tell us as
much about him as any of the information in his play-length monologue; he
needs someone to whom he can address his remarks. He would like to think in
his arrogance that he is his own director and playwright, but Fornes makes it
clear that he is as controlled by drama as the rest of us.

Textually, Dr. Kheal, a professor, is indeed his own narrator; he tells us his
own story and controls his audience insofar as he can withhold information or
embellish it at his will. As he asserts, he is "the master" (129), which he illustrates in his attitude toward his audience. The play's form is that of a professor's
lecture, and the audience, therefore, is cast as Dr. Kheal's students. Though he
addresses questions to these students, dictums of theatrical behavior (politeness)
prevent any response. Hence, Dr. Kheal never bothers to wait for an answer

and successfully makes the audience superfluous to his performance on the textual level of questioning and answering.

Dr. Kheal eventually undermines the sense of his mastery of the audience
by presenting himself as an exhibitionist, an object for the audience's
voyeurism. It becomes increasingly clear that it is the audience that makes his
articulations worthwhile for him, that enables his performance and his lyricism.
At the very least he needs to pretend to ask questions of his students in order to
answer them himself. His comprehension of the nature of the theater in that
context is ironic at best:

> There is poetry. . . . But who, tell me, understands the poetry of space in a
> box? I do. . . . Abysmal and concrete at the same time. Four walls, a top, and
> a bottom . . . and yet a void. . . . Who understands that? I, Professor Kheal, I
> understand it clearly and expound it well! (130)

The four walls of this particular theatrical event do not entirely separate Dr.
Kheal from his spectators; for that matter, he acknowledges that he needs those
spectators precisely for this particular expounding.

Dr. Kheal's relationship with his audience is as tentative as his relationship
with the sexual foil Fornes provides him with—significantly, a foil only he can
see (one might say that Dr. Kheal is the only one in the theater who can see his
audience, at least en masse or as a single entity). Dr. Kheal "sees Crissanda in
front of him" (133), puts words in her mouth, then makes clear that the relationship dissolved because of his own ineptitude; he had abused his power over
her by laughing at her, upset their particular balance, which he defines as "a
state of equilibrium between opposing forces. . . . Balance is keeping my pants
up" (130). His behavior with Crissanda is the paradigm for his behavior with his
audience, and from the play's start he threatens to abuse *that* power. Powerless
as the spectators are, Dr. Kheal will be the one to upset the equilibrium should
it come to that.

Despite his pomposity, Fornes eventually awards Dr. Kheal a genuine sen-
sitivity. He is as vulnerable as anyone else to the fragility of his own arrogance.
He knows that reality and love are "opposites, contradictions compressed so
that you don't know where one stops and the other begins" (134); that is, he
knows that there is no such thing as true independence and separateness. He
offers a confession and apology, encompassed by the image he draws for the
audience of his concept of hope. Though the image illustrates Dr. Kheal's continued attempts to distinguish himself from his audience, it also reveals his
understanding that his greatest obstacle is the theater itself and that the audience

is therefore also responsible for his manners of acting therein. Dr. Kheal's hope is for the opposite of "being enclosed," for "freedom, open space, air, sun" (134), which is ultimately hope for freedom from the theater, even from the beautiful "lyrical thing" of "the poetry of space in a box." The theater, in the end, is for Dr. Kheal a "grotto" (134) from which he hungers to escape, because within theatrical space he can never be free of the other, of his audience.

Dr. Kheal's characterization of the restrictions theatrical space puts on one's character, as it were, is idiosyncratic and controlled by his own ego. For Dr. Kheal "Man," who can see the beauty in brussels sprouts (134), is the "superior beast" and "the rational animal" (135) and, as such, is fated to abuse power by virtue of being able to talk down to his audience. Inadvertently, however, Dr. Kheal's vision of hope is really a vision of a world in which he might not feel compelled to exercise his own power. Dr. Kheal assumes that we are confined to play whatever roles we are competent to play. What he does not imagine is that a world might exist in which he would be free of his own arrogance, a world in which he would not be cornered into any role—rather, a world in which he could choose his own role, based not on any inherent powers but on reasoned desire. In that world he could be welcome to his audience without needing to abuse them.

Fornes's revelry becomes increasingly burdened from *Dr. Kheal* onward. *Fefu and Her Friends* (1978) provides a bridge to Fornes's later work—plays more endowed with politics, plays with social conscience: *The Danube* (1982), *Mud* (1983), *Sarita* (1984), *Abingdon Square* (1984), *The Conduct of Life* (1985), and *What of the Night?* (1993).[1] Fornes's characters become more complex sexually, socially, politically, economically; they are characters created by their contexts, as are those described earlier, but by contexts of increasing sophistication, foregrounded theatrical contexts that simultaneously mimic the larger world: respectively, women's issues, Eastern Europe, poverty, the Hispanic South Bronx, wealth and education, the political oppression of Latin America, and gender politics.

In Fornes's later plays roles transcend the theater, via the theater, to the social and political theater of the real world. While *Fefu,* for example, is still about making theater, it is more intricately about what productive roles women might play in the lives of other women. As in many of Fornes's later plays, through *Fefu* Fornes continues to delineate the despotism of both political and artistic structures. In *Mud* and *Sarita* Fornes uses the theater as a physical image to represent context in general—social, economic, political—and the heroines of those two plays suffer a violence engendered by their repressive contexts. Ubiquitously, Fornes's characters become more human even while Fornes investigates the dehumanization of humanity that both politics and art can propagate—*The Danube*'s pivotal concern.

The Danube is haunted by forces on the one hand peripheral to its drama—offstage, minimally imaged, abstract—and on the other hand fundamentally determining of the drama's crisis. Eve and Paul try to pursue a romance within the larger contexts, and constraints, of a world deteriorating under the influence of something resembling a nuclear holocaust, and within the less daunting but also powerful world of the theater. That happiness will elude them is a foregone conclusion nearly from the start, both because of the ominous and alienating world they inhabit (Hungary in the 1930s or 1940s, but only vaguely—time and place are distorted as soon as the drama gets under way) and, theatrically, because of the intense formality to which Fornes confines their discourse. Paul and Eve's romance is scripted by language tapes that either precede or succeed their articulations but, in either case, bind their articulations to the most simple and banal language:

> *Paul:* Are you a good cook, Miss Sandor?
> *Eve:* I am . . . a good cook. Do you like to cook, Mr. Green?
> *Paul:* I am not a very good cook. I only know how to make eggs, toast, boiled potatoes and a steak. What forms of entertainment are there in Budapest, Miss Sandor? (47)

Their courtship is made up entirely of such exchanges, which formalizes their budding romance. Yet it is precisely the formality of their exchanges that evokes subtext; clearly, language distances these characters from the truth of their feelings, even from what they really want to say.

When scene changes are rounded with smoke rising from the stage floor or when "plaintive music" (50) provides a score for their exchanges, the theater—or theatrical spectacle—becomes the undisputable controlling force. At certain moments in the drama, holocaust and theater emerge. The world-gone-wrong is illustrated in scene 10, for example, by an "amorphous black object" in Paul's coffee cup, inexplicably wet cigarettes, nonsensical references to weather and season, and finally skewed time—a single day passes in an instant before the audience's eyes. Fornes takes theatrical liberties not merely to illustrate the chaos and destruction of the surrounding world; in fact, the allusions to holocaust, to disease and despair, may be illustration for the chaos of *The Danube*'s theater. The last few scenes of the play are enacted twice, once by the characters and once by the puppets the characters manipulate, effectively confusing the direction of metaphor. The puppet play—that is, the imaging of the theatrical experience once removed—suggests that the theater is as much to blame for this tragedy as any political or environmental cause about which we might conjecture. The puppet play forces the audience to focus on the art itself as a destructive force.

Distinctions between the power of language and of theater further obscure the source of villainy. Even as the characters become increasingly ill—reduced to vomiting, fainting, sleeping—even as they fall more and more victim to holocaust, they become more literate, resembling less and less the parroting mannequins of the earlier acts. The play's greatest tragedy is that the characters' increasing aptitude for language, their increasing ability to communicate, does not actually forge connections between them. On the one hand, language can bring these characters (and their audience, for that matter) closer to the truth of subtext, such as when Paul first uses Eve's name, breaking out of the patter of the language tapes to say, "Eve, come with me to a cafe. There's one not far from my hotel" (49), or when Eve first uses Paul's name—"Paul. . . . Are you leaving Budapest?" (50)—revealing her sadness and prompting his marriage proposal. These moments take on remarkable weight, become virtually erotic in their difference and boldness, and remind the spectator that Eve and Paul's romance is occurring on a different level than their words have otherwise indicated. But these brief literary transcendences, like the characters' increasingly poetic articulations in general, belie language's sweeping inadequacies. Their textual lives have been obscuring their more true theatrical lives. While the theater is partially responsible for their entrapment, it is also what may save them.

The play's final scene, during which the audience knows that all the characters' deaths are imminent and inevitable even while those characters insist they will flee Hungary, repeats almost verbatim the penultimate scene enacted with puppets. What distinguishes scene 15 from scene 14, however, is what Fornes adds, both textually and theatrically. Mr. Green, Eve's father, is given more lines, which he uses to explain his unwillingness to leave his country: "I live here and work here. My family lives here. . . . It doesn't matter, Eve. There's no place to go" (64). Fornes also adds a gun to the props on the stage, taking full advantage of the theater's capacity to move beyond the text, to change the dramatic world to a theatrical, image-able world, to provide theatrical tension. She suggests that their human theater can be significantly more potent than their puppet theater. Though the gun is never used in the course of this particular drama, its presence points to the theatrical power that has not been exploited, a power that might considerably illuminate the inner lives of these characters.

The theater illustrates the moment of Paul and Eve's deaths with a "brilliant white flash of light" before the final blackout (64). When Eve tries to exit the stage with Paul, the theater holds them in the end through that final image. Despite the play's apparent optimism about the theater's potential to effect change, to shape character, this drama is devastatingly cynical in its homage to the contexts we cannot escape—the languages we are forced to use, the stages we walk on, the deterioration of our natural world—bowing, finally, to the power of context over the power of the individual.

With *Fefu and Her Friends, The Danube* marks Fornes's increasingly meticulous consideration of the theater both as powerful in its own right and as an especially complicated metaphor for the limited and limiting contexts imposed by art, nature, and humanity. The lyricism of both the dramas and the theatrical environments to come is composed of more anguished struggles between characters, more dangerous props, and more menacing stage spaces. *Fefu* in effect picks up where *The Danube* lets off; there is also a gun on the stage, but this time that "device" will be used to its full theatrical advantage.

Fefu and Her Friends is a watershed in Fornes's career, though on either side of that play Fornes has intently used the theater as a genuinely real place. What happens to bodies on the stage happens to real bodies; the audience's response to the activity on the stage is always a potentially productive response. In her later plays the consequences of theatrical participation, for characters on and off the stage, become more ominous as they become more distinct. Each of the following chapters pursues that theme as it pervades Fornes's major plays.

Fefu and Her Friends

Fefu and Her Friends, first produced in 1977 by the New York Theatre Strategy at the Relativity Media Lab—in its dressing room, its kitchen, and business office as well as on its stage—offers the most minimal of plots, with one singular exception. Eight women gather in 1935 to plan a theatrical event about education. They do not get around to discussing it much until the third act, distracted as they are in the first two acts with themselves, their relationships to one another, lunch, and tea. *Fefu* recalls the previous decade's *Promenade* and *Tango Palace* in its emphasis on character above story and on its characters' self-absorption. But this play's form retains only hints of absurdism and reenters the realm of realistic representation even while sustaining formal experimentation in order to work more directly with the woman as theatrical subject. The play climaxes with a violent but inconclusive confrontation between Fefu and the wheelchair-bound Julia, as each woman struggles for her place on this stage.

The play's lyricism results in part from its status as a map of contradictions between what characters say and what their presences' communicate, what they and their audience think may be happening and what certain evidence suggests may be otherwise. To *listen* to these characters is often to hear insecurity, fear, and tentativeness, while to *look at* them is to see a community of women variously empowering one another. Fefu, the play's ostensible protagonist, is the paradigm of these multitextual characterizations. Although Fefu implies that she likes men better than women, the emotional distance between her and her husband is immeasurable, and by the play's end she has sincerely thanked almost every woman in her home for what each has enabled in her. The text she writes with her body is also fraught with contradiction. Fefu has gathered these women in her home, and she acts the nervous host, pacing her house, entering and exiting rooms in the middle of conversations, leaving trails of non sequiturs behind her. She is also the physical center of her theatrical space; the movements of the other women in her home revolve conspicuously around Fefu's movements, whether or not she is on the stage.

In fact, the play is as much about those carefully choreographed movements, virtual dance routines, as anything else—certainly more about those physical and emotional meanderings than the presentation that serves to have brought the women together but demands little attention, either from them or from the audience. The elusiveness of the play's exact focus is further assisted by the lack of dramatic hierarchy. While the most intense dramatic action in the play involves two of the characters, Fefu and Julia, each of the other characters has her own drama that both intersects Fefu's and Julia's and exists independently. And the climactic moment between Fefu and Julia is not necessarily the play's most illuminating nor significant. The theatrical environment resembles the spontaneity of a workshop: one character speaks, another responds, another enters the room, has her effect, and so on. What matters are all of those moments. Indeed, *Fefu* is most famous for its second act, which is staged in four different rooms for the audience divided into four sections. Hence, each section of audience will see a different play; one will see a drama in which an image of a hallucinating Julia is followed by Fefu describing her devotion to a sickly cat; another will see Julia's scene followed by two ex-lovers trying to avoid speaking their anger to each other, and so on. The overall experience for the spectators will be that the order of events is random; we cannot read this play through conventional dramatic techniques of rising action and peripeteia, for example. The experience of progress is illusory; it may all add up but in the way that a collage does rather than as a linear narrative.

The tensions between Fefu's concurrent texts, her physical and emotional contradictions, mimic that structure of collage. She is simultaneously many things: arrogant and insecure, elusive and focal, powerful and powerless. Her dichotomies reverberate for all of the women in this drama and maybe for all of the women in the audience as well. Particular feminist significance comes from *Fefu*'s position within a debate about what constitutes a female subject. Materialist and culturalist feminist movements maintain that "woman" on the stage is a construct or fiction. In *The Feminist Spectator as Critic* (1988), Jill Dolan theorizes: "An image of a woman cannot merely denote. . . . Placing women in a representation always connotes an underlying ideology and presents a narrative driven by male desire that effectively denies women's subjectivity" (57); and, again, "the female body is not reducible to a sign free of connotation. Women always bear the mark and meaning of their sex, which inscribes them within a cultural hierarchy" (63). For Dolan, because "realist theater imposes a conservative sense of order by delivering its ideology as normative" (106), realist conventions must be exposed to undermine their capacity to seduce the spectator into accepting representation as truth. Fornes responds as if to a challenge, threatening that "cultural hierarchy" with erasure: by peopling her stage with only women's bodies engaged in narrative and physical action, sometimes realistic, sometimes marked by alienation techniques, she invites her spectators to accept her characters as subjects intact.

In *Fefu* Fornes explores the powers of voice and presence of individual women (the different stories each can tell), and their counterparts in text and theatricality, in order to illustrate how they can collaborate to provide a stage for her female subjects—and, by implication, for the empathic spectator in the audience. This is a theatrical enterprise above all else but with (in)direct consequences even for those not of this theatrical event. Essentially, Fornes insists that the female subject can exist in the theater and, if there, then also elsewhere. Deborah R. Geis notes that "nearly all of the monologues in *Fefu*, up to Emma's lecture, dwell on the characters' sense of identity as defined in relationship to (or, more accurately, in contradiction to) their view of men" (1990, 296). Hence, for Geis it is not until the "play's third act [that it] invites a possible re-inscription [of subjectivity] on [the women's] own terms" (298), while I see that re-inscription happening throughout in the women's utter domination of the stage space; their subjectivity is repeatedly authenticated through the very inconsistency of their presences. Stacy Wolf also reads this quite differently than I do. By making a distinction between "images (i.e., content) . . . [and] form" (1992, 17), she supports rigid dichotomies of masculine and feminine for which I do not find support in Fornes's characterizations. Wolf quotes Teresa de Lauretis—"The representation of violence is inseparable from the notion of gender" (1987, 36)—and then uncritically reads power and powerlessness as masculine and feminine positions in turn. With no masculine presence on the stage, I find that dichotomy unproductive for Fornes's spectators. Guileless or not, Fornes simply ignores the binary masculine-feminine division by keeping men from the drama.

While men are not heard from, Fornes amplifies the women's voices by providing context for each with careful theatrical framing: *Fefu*'s stage is a women's stage, constructed as such both thematically and formally. Though the women repeatedly describe their conflicts with men, on this stage the conflicts are confined to the women. Alternatively, W. B. Worthen suggests that "the authority of the absent male is everywhere evident" (1989, 176), which Stacy Wolf amends to read, "the authority of the 'violent male' is everywhere evident." Wolf also suggests that "Fornes's spare characterizations prevent the spectator from placing each woman's violent story within the context of her life. Her story not only emblematizes her character—it is her character, with her entire subjectivity signified by this one violent act, wherein it remains unanalyzed" (25). While these readings may bear out some thematic accuracy (though Wolf's is overstated), they do not approach the issue of the visual texts' contradiction of the women's narrative texts. I see a crucial distinction between Worthen's and Wolf's "evident" and actual presence in this particular dramatic world; the stage remains the women's. The existence of men in the lives of these women, outside of this theater, need not be denied, but the influences of men and their social and economic potency pass through the conduit of the women's understanding of these influences; here the women are self-narrated. The play suggests the means by which these self-narrated women might work together to reconstitute their own subjectivity, to gain enough self-knowledge and self-awareness to enable genuine self-control or, finally, self-dramatization.

The spectator's experience of *Fefu* is a ubiquitous self-consciousness similar to the characters'. The steady perception of the set as an assemblage is heightened by the spectator's act of wandering through those sets; the awareness of the characters as characters is heightened by the spectator's unusual proximity to the characters, the entering into their space, but still only as spectators. Helene Keyssar deduces from her own experience as a spectator of *Fefu* that "the audience is disconcerted . . . we are *in* their spaces but not of them. Their world remains separate from ours, and there is nothing we can do to make a difference. . . . [I]n each viewing of each scene of *Fefu* our position as audience members is re-accentuated and our relationship to the characters is re-mediated" (1991, 100). If we actively experience this re-mediation, we enable the possibility of a forum for these voices outside this event.

The spectator's keen sense of his or her role in relation to this dramatization is underscored further by the play's deliberate theatricalization of character, each one framed as a character in a drama rather than representative of a "real" woman. Some of the characters in this drama show awareness of the powers of self-theatricalization: they recognize their words as a script that an audience must listen to and their presences as images that an audience must confront; hence, these characters seek to theatricalize their selves in order to surmount the roles in which they have been cast. Fornes's eclectic approach to form is particularly rewarding for the women in this play; the lyrical space resulting from realism and the simultaneous exploding of realism creates an elastic theatrical territory. In order to explore women characters' presence in particular, Fornes offers a theatrical space especially sensitive to the theater's potential as an alternative space, part real, part fiction. The spectator is drawn into the actual theatrical space, and the climactic conflict between Fefu and Julia is metatheatrical, specifically in order to violate the distinctions between the real and the fictive. The eight women characters' various struggles to inhabit this "female" space account for almost all the dramatic and narrative action. Julia's highly theatrical "hallucinations"; Fefu's repeated rehearsal of the theatrical component of her marriage to Phillip; the rehearsal of the feminist presentation on education for which the women have gathered; the staging of relationships among the women; the divisions into roles of actors, spectators, and critics *within* the drama; and the obscuring of the roles of actors and spectators around the drama all conspire to realize a theatrical space especially designed for the representation of female subjects. Finally, Fornes makes use of this special space to foreground women's voices and presence. Ultimately, even by acknowledging that presence as theatrical, she suggests the possibility of that presence in the realm of the real. The theater, if not the world beyond the theater, becomes a substantial, material place in which these characters can be women.

Part 1 of *Fefu and Her Friends* immediately establishes that this play will be concerned with women's issues—the ways in which women talk together, the ways they organize and inhabit their spaces, their relationships with both women and men. The play's initial frame is structured by three women, one standing, one lying down, one sitting; in this revised image of Chekhov's three sisters their language is neither romantic nor nostalgic, even if their postures, and ultimately their central concerns, are similar. Fefu opens with: "My husband married me to have a constant reminder of how loathsome women are. . . . He tells me constantly" (112). A woman quoting a man, using his language, establishes the sides of a warfare (accented by the shotgun incongruously placed in a room decorated with a "tasteful mixture of styles" [112]) that will be characterized by a struggle between an active and a passive voice. Fefu and Cindy's conversation is itself a conversation between an active and a passive voice, echoing what Fefu has suggested is the paradigm of her marriage; that same dichotomy has spread into the women's discourse. But Fornes uses the comparison not merely to indicate the oppression of the passive by the active but also to indicate what might be compelled in an active character when confronted with another's passivity. As Keyssar asserts, "Often, one or another of the women does not understand each other, but what one says to another changes the other before our eyes" (1991, 99). The act of conversation destabilizes our sense of a character as a fixed entity; representation itself undergoes constant transformation. Cindy intersperses Fefu's assertions with: "That's just awful. . . . It isn't awful? . . . I don't think anyone would marry for that reason. . . . Oh dear." Fefu, up against Cindy's acquiescence, plays her husband's role. "It's funny—And it's true," she says, embracing that particular male perspective. "That's why I laugh" (113). At this juncture Fefu does not make clear her subject: Is it the content of Phillip's sentiment whose truth she embraces or simply that it is, in fact, Phillip's opinion? Fefu is not being guileful; she is undergoing the process of thought.

Fefu defends her still ambiguous stance by insisting that the assertion that women are loathsome is an exciting idea because it is so revolting. Fefu is manipulating language but apparently in order to prevent her friends from making facile conclusions either about her or her marriage or, by extension, about themselves. She asks Cindy and Christina to remember a time when they have turned over a stone:

> You see, that which is exposed to the exterior . . . is smooth and dry and clean. That which is not . . . underneath, is slimy and filled with fungus and crawling with worms. It is another life that is parallel to the one we manifest. It's there. The way worms are underneath the stone. If you don't recognize it . . . it eats you. (114)

If we do not confront the ugly truth, Fefu asserts, then we are trapped in the illusion of cleanliness. This house—this set—looks nice but is not necessarily. And the same may be said of their friendships. The danger may be within themselves.

Fittingly, this seemingly conclusive statement from Fefu points not to the consequences of thinking as she does (i.e., she is not spared the self-loathing her relationship with Phillip inspires) but, rather, to the necessity of allowing thought to undergo process. The spectator, with Christina and Cindy, is subjected to an insecure experience of initial responses to Fefu's comments, quickly altered by her linguistically playful if ominous follow-ups. Fefu's meaning changes moment to moment: she means, first, that she is amused by her husband's having this idea, then that it is funny that women are loathsome, then that women are loathsome, then not that individual women are loathsome but that "It's something to grapple with" (114). This is a process of, as Fornes has told Scott Cummings, thoughts becoming words that undergo a constant distortion even while reaching articulation. Fefu cannot be judged by her speech alone (if we do so, as Christina threatens to do, she will "take it all back"), as will become increasingly true as she successfully and intelligently contradicts herself throughout the play.

We must not judge Fefu by her actions alone either, which will also bear considerable contradictions as she plays out both absolute control and absolute vulnerability. Fefu follows her reference to the repugnant life beneath an over-turned stone with an explicitly theatrical seizing of the drama: she "shoots" Phillip, who is out on the lawn. Within seconds the audience knows that it is a game, that the gun is not loaded but that Phillip will fall every time Fefu shoots. But, by not knowing the truth immediately, the illusion of Fefu's control of this stage (physically begun with her standing, while the other two women lie and sit) is insinuated further just as she leaves the stage. Cindy and Christina remind the spectators both of their responsibility and their unstable positions at this moment by acting as critics; they try to analyze Fefu, though they do not get far. Their analysis is superficial, given their lack of real information about the details of Fefu's life or marriage: "She's unique. There's no one like her. . . . But she is lovely you know. . . . She's crazy. . . . She has a strange marriage" (115), and so on. And they turn the stone back over before they have come to any real truths: Christina says, "Put the gun away, I don't like looking at it. . . . That shawl. Put it over the gun" (116).

Fefu returns to the stage, having just controlled space elsewhere, that is, fixing the house's plumbing. To Christina's "You do your own plumbing?" Fefu's explicit and direct reply is, of course, but her implicit reply, moments later, is: "He scared me this time you know. He looked like he was really hurt," suggesting that they withhold their respect for her maintenance skills at least temporarily. Now Fefu admits to her theatricality; Phillip has really been controlling these events, she avers: "He told me one day he'll put real bullets in the gun" (116). She needs Phillip to be in control, Fefu says, because otherwise she would be accountable for her actions and "might shoot him for real" (117). She suggests that the status quo is a kind of compromise, though the audience is in a position to wonder to what extent that compromise only creates the illusion of shared control of this theatrical game, since Phillip is always the one loading the gun. Stacy Wolf suggests that "Fefu's desire for Phillip . . . disempowers her as soon as she shoots the gun, and she slips into a feminized gender location" (1992, 27); I find, however, that the illusion of control threatens that conclusion, as does Phillip's ultimate vulnerability: Fefu may become a murderer, but it is Phillip's life which is in danger.

Though Fefu has indicated that her self-control is jeopardized, or at least mediated, by Phillip, she can still effectively banish him from this drama. *This* stage is not Phillip's. He is offstage—and doomed to be offstage throughout the entire production. In the context of these relationships between women, Fefu truly has the stage. She manipulates Christina into having a second bourbon, just as she manipulates both Cindy and Christina into accepting her despite all the misgivings and fears she inspires in them. Fefu accounts for her power over herself and others by insisting that her stance is virile. Standing in the doorway, framed there, Fefu says: "I like being like a man. Thinking like a man. Feeling like a man," but Fornes hints at the tenuousness of that posture. This is acting, this is theater, while Phillip is out in the real world, "checking the new grass mower. . . . Out in the fresh air and the sun, while we sit here in the dark" (117).

In part Fefu is suggesting that women choose theatrical lives specifically in order to avoid the intensity of their real lives. Ironically, in the context of the power of the theater as a whole, at this moment Fefu describes the women's (theatrical) world as a retreat: a dark place that defies clear vision, where one will not be able to see the underside of the stone. Fefu says that women use men to keep distance between themselves, between women—use men as "muscle that cover the raw nerve . . . [as] insulators. . . . But the price is the mind and the spirit" (118). She shifts the discourse from relations between women and men to relations between women and women. Women choose theatricality, Fefu insinuates, as a way of keeping distance from themselves and from one another.

Fefu then asks disingenuously, "What is the fear?" though she has already made that clear. The fear is of being known ("as if a god once said 'and if they shall recognize each other, the world will be blown apart'" [118]), of having one's darkness, the underside of the stone, exposed. If women were genuinely to seize control of their space—of the spaces that only women inhabit, the spaces into which men are not invited, the space of this particular theatrical event—they might frighten themselves and their spectators away.[1] But, most important, what Fefu ultimately implies here is that women can choose theatricality as a way of providing themselves access to the real. Once they are responsible for their own theatricality, they make it harder for others to make a spectacle out of them.

Christina and Cindy waylay progress for the time being by avoiding the truth. Christina misunderstands Fefu. Though Fefu has said that women use men to keep distance from one another and even from themselves, "to feel safe," Christina makes a connection that Fefu does not imply. "I too have wished for that trust men have for each other," she says. Christina is assuming that Fefu thinks that women will use knowledge of one another as power over one another—and, in turn, will hurt one another. Christina covets "the faith the world puts in [men] and they in turn put in the world," coveting what Fefu knows is blind faith, not necessarily earned by intimacy or genuine familiarity with the individual. Being known, Christina assumes, will be what wards off others' faith; even the bare threat of being known has hurt her. In response to Fefu's honesty and directness, Christina says: "I hurt. I'm all shreds inside" (118). So Fefu, with only a "Hmm," is off to her plumbing again, leaving Cindy to comfort Christina in a manner Fefu never would. Cindy sings a lullaby, smoothing over the pain instead of confronting it.

Into the midst of these unsatisfactory communications comes Julia in a wheelchair. At this point in the drama Julia is the physical dramatization of the emotionally disabled women she is joining. Julia is the victim of an inexplicable accident in which a hunter shot a deer and Julia fell, though she was not hit by any bullet. The accident caused paralysis and hallucinations, particularly about male persecutors. Cindy, resistant as she is to the theater's capacity to refigure, needs to believe there is a "realistic" explanation for the events of Julia's disabling. She wants to name Julia's disease ("It's a scar in the brain. It's called the petit mal") and asserts that, if it was not the hunter, or Fefu, then "it was someone else" who shot Julia. She explains to Christina that she has not talked about what Julia said when she was delirious because she "fear[s] for her." Julia had said:

> That she was persecuted.—That they tortured her. . . . That they had tried her and that the shot was her execution. That she recanted because she wanted to live. . . . That if she talked about it . . . to anyone . . . she would be tortured and killed. (119)

Cindy's explanation for her own silence makes no sense: From what is she protecting Julia by not responding to her? While Cindy focuses on what Julia has come to fear, obviously overwhelmed herself by that threat, Fefu focuses on how fearful Julia has become. "You remember her then how she was," she says. "She was afraid of nothing. . . . She knew so much." The implication of Fefu's concern is that, although there will always be something to fear, one must master fear for the sake of knowledge and experience, for the sake of being alive. But for Christina Julia's accident is about vulnerability: "We are made of putty," she says. "Aren't we?" (119). Neither Cindy nor Christina can see beyond that susceptibility. For them Julia is the theatricalization of the human body always vulnerable, always subject to pain. For Fefu, Julia is the danger of her own word made literal, of her unwillingness to defy the text with her presence. Julia's fear—before, during, and after the accident—has been her crippling.

Offstage noises mark a break in the scene accompanied by the entry of a new character who seems meant to balance, with Fefu, the "weaknesses" of the other three women, in terms both of personality—that kind of presence—and the impact of her particular theatrical presence. Emma is loud and aggressive, spectacularly dressed, assertive, and funny. Emma and Fefu embrace and are both expressive and intimate. Emma is not wary around Julia; she jumps into her lap, demanding a ride. And Emma is the first to refer to the upcoming presentation as theater: "We should do a rehearsal in costume," she says. "What color should each wear. It matters" (120).

Emma voices the important assertion that distinctions between life and theater are false. In response to Sue's "I had no idea we were going to do theatre," Emma answers:

> Life is theatre. Theatre is life. If we're showing what life is, can be, we must do theatre. . . . It's not acting. It's being. It's springing forth with the powers of the spirit. It's breathing. (121)

In the theater, Emma suggests, time as we know it collapses: refiguring the present within the theater is as productive as living the present outside the theater. She justifies the emphasis of form over content by intimating the importance of the visual image through which passes the message. Their presences alone can show what "can be."

"I'm happy," Emma concludes, having asserted that fundamental truth. And Julia responds, "I'll do a dance" (121). This may be sarcasm at its most pure, confined as she is to a wheelchair, or it may be the quintessence of hope, that is, a temporary belief in the transformative power of the theater as described by Emma. But then Julia adds, "I'm game," ostensibly to dancing, but we know she is game already. According to her, she is the victim of someone else's play, someone's sport, and so her words ring with accusation. She could be warning Emma of the more dangerous powers of theater, of acting out, so to speak. And the sport she indirectly refers to must recall Fefu and Phillip's sport. Who is their victim? What will be the repercussions of their theatrical game?

Part 1 ends on pure theatricality, a spotlight on a new and as yet unknowable character. Julia has fallen into a trance after handling Fefu's gun, and Cindy has picked up the gun off the floor to reload the blank slug. Cecilia enters, introduces herself, and the lights fade around her, leaving her the sole focus. It may be that this so purposely directed spotlight on a stranger is meant to reenforce how finally strange is all that we think we know to this point. Though the women assembled in Fefu's house act familiarly, even comfortably with one another, Fefu and the entire theatrical narrative have prepared the audience for its disillusionment. The dramatic peak marked by Cecilia's entrance is somewhat artificial; her presence resolves no mysteries and furthers no story. Rather, closing part 1 on this note opens up the play both narratively and theatrically. And, as Cecilia proves to be no more pivotal a character than any other, in retrospect particularly, her entrance does little more than randomly push the drama in a new direction.

Each of part 2's vignettes is to some extent about women's intimacy, though each also evokes the characters' dissatisfaction and feelings of incompleteness. Whether a scene will be a lens or a commentary on another scene in part 2 will be different for individual spectators.[2] The representation of the lesbian relationship between Cecilia and Paula will provide either introduction or conclusion to the relationship between Fefu and Emma, as will Cindy's dream for Julia's hallucinations. (Julia and Cindy do evoke W. B. Worthen's "absent men," though provocatively *only* as hallucination and dream.) The scenes' simultaneity, as did Fefu's thought process in the first act, suggests that cursory distinctions between friendship and romance, for example, or justified fear and paranoia will be challenged. Each scene, finally, represents women's characters-in-process—Helene Keyssar finds in part 2 a dramatization of Fornes's representation of multiple points of view (100)—specifically, character as constructed by interaction with other women or, in Julia's case particularly and for the others implicitly, by the explicit relationship of the self with one's audience.

In "On the Lawn" Emma and Fefu are spotlighted outdoors, in the "male world," as Fefu indicated in part 1, though here too there are no men. Though these two women would be likely to speak frankly about sex in any context, this particular space seems especially to have enabled their conversation to take place (perhaps because of their relative privacy from the other women). Emma opens with, "Do you think about genitals all the time?" From there they engage playfully in discussion, concluding somewhat indirectly that sex is a moral issue— for women, at least. "In heaven," Emma insists, "they don't judge goodness the way we think." She continues:

> They have a divine registry of sexual performance. In that registry they mark down every little sexual activity in your life. If your faith is not entirely in it, if you just perform as an obligation and you don't feel the most profound devotion, if your spirit, your heart and your flesh, is not religiously delivered to it, you are condemned. (122)

Fefu elaborates, "On earth we are judged by public acts, and sex is a private act" (123). On the one hand, Fefu suggests that she and others who are sexually "faithful" do not receive the proper credit for their piety. On the other hand, she seems confident that her true virtue will be rewarded in heaven.

Although Emma and Fefu's exchange sounds honest and mutually reen-forcing and even inspires Fefu to say, "You always bring joy to me," their con-nection is incomplete and inadequate; they cannot cure each other. Fefu tells Emma about her spiritual pain ("it's not sorrow"), which entails a sense of responsibility toward the uglier elements of her world, specifically toward the black cat who comes into her kitchen and fouls it with diarrhea. Fefu admits that she cannot turn the cat away, despite her repulsion, though she does not suggest that it is compassion that directs her. "At first I was repelled by him," she says, "but then, I thought, this is a monster that has been sent to me and I must feed him. . . . I still feed him. I am afraid of him" (123). Her pain appears to stem from willfully overcoming her disgust but at the cost of accentuating her fear (which should recall Julia's experience of men). She is neither loving nor helping the cat but accommodating it without analysis. Even the honesty and optimism encompassed in her exchange with Emma are not a match for what is missing in Fefu; she is not making the connecting leap between her actions and her motivations. Is her feeding the cat, for example, an effort to sustain some aspect of herself? Or to punish herself? Does her tending the cat amount to the kind of private act that will eventually redeem her? Or is her tending the cat a passively rebellious act for Fefu, a way of giving up control of her space as Julia had done?

As a whole, the scene raises the question of whether an honest link with another enables honesty with oneself. Emma, at least, indirectly answers yes. When Fefu leaves the stage, Emma recites Shakespeare's fourteenth sonnet, which concludes:

> . . . from thine eyes my knowledge I derive,
> And, constant stars, in them I read such art
> As truth and beauty shall together thrive
> If from thyself to store though wouldst convert:
>   Or else of thee this prognosticate,
>   Thy end is truth's and beauty's doom and date.
>
> (123)

Emma's response, however, is by no means conclusive, as not only Fefu's behavior but also the behavior of the other women illustrate.

Christina and Cindy's scene, "In the Study," offers another poem of sorts in the flow and construction of their discourse, particularly in the sense of end rhymes; Cindy's dream works as commentary on Christina's anxiety about Fefu. The gist of Christina's concern is her fear of what Fefu's "adventurousness" may threaten in others, particularly in herself. She is afraid of Fefu's ability to disturb surfaces. Cindy's dream describes a similar anxiety, though, compellingly, an anxiety about men's power. Fefu's powers are more and more aligned with men's by Cindy and Christina and later by Julia. All of their fear has to do with what exists beyond their control and the truths they are or will be unable to elude. Cindy's dream is about being "cured," helped, or corrected, all of which, barely indirectly, mean being hurt. To some extent her dream mimics Julia's hallucinations, though the form of a dream mediates any sense of paranoia. But the dream also comments on what Christina has said about Fefu:

> I don't know if she's careful with life. . . . Her mind is adventurous. I don't
> know if there is dishonesty in that. But in adventure there is taking chances
> and risk, and then one has to, somehow, have less regard or respect for things
> as they are. (125)

Fefu, of course, would embrace Christina's remarks as the highest flattery, but the questions Christina raises about Fefu's honesty cannot be ignored. If Christina is referring to Fefu and Phillip's game, then she is pointing out that, while their efforts to disrupt the status quo may be admirable, the repercussions are unpredictable and potentially very dangerous.

Cindy's dream, which she uses to answer Christina's concerns, isolates the issue of power's potential destructiveness. When in her dream Cindy is unable to control her own language ("Then, I said to [the male doctor], 'Restrain yourself.' I wanted to say respect me" [125]), the doctor responds with violent rage; Cindy's life is threatened. Cindy's dream is cast with a number of male authority figures—a doctor, a policeman, a professor, a husband or male lover—who appear to be helpful but, instead, threaten great harm. Succeeding Christina's outline of her discomfort with Fefu, the dream is meant to show Cindy's sympathy with Christina. Cindy implies that the danger that Fefu poses is like the danger that men often pose not by being men but by abusing authority. As in part 1, Cindy and Christina's fear of Fefu pertains to the violence they fear Fefu might do with knowledge and power.

Both women reveal—Christina through her tentative language and Cindy through that detail of her dream that locates her sense of a lack of control within herself ("I wanted to say respect me" but was unable to)—the extent to which Fefu's power frightens them, particularly because of their own gaps in power. Fefu, they admit, has not taken anything from them. Stage directions indicate that Fefu's entrance into the study "may interrupt Cindy's speech at any point according to how long it takes her to reach the kitchen" (126); that is, that particular narrative does not require closure. (Fefu's entrance in the midst of Cindy's dream will further the audience's sense of her alignment with dangerous male authority.) But Christina's response to Cindy has already rendered moot any closure; she has only been listening on the surface. "I think [the dream] means you should go to a different doctor," she says carelessly, and, when Cindy apparently asks for more ("He's not my doctor. I never saw him before"), Christina offers nothing further. "Well good," she says. "I'm sure he's not a good doctor" (126). Christina fears honesty to the extent that she cannot even receive it from a friend, even when she is not implicated in any crime. Her method of repression is denial and reticence, but the results differ little from, for example, Fefu's unwillingness to reason out her fears or Julia's transference onto others.

Julia's scene, "In the Bedroom," stands in relief because it is dominated by a single voice, though a voice apparently engaged in a dialogue disguised as hallucination. The audience is not only in the room but standing around Julia's bed, virtually forced into a peculiar violation of her privacy. If the audience members are not explicitly cast as the muted participants in this dialogue, they are, at the very least, "witnesses."[3] And, as such, their obligation is to the truth, whether that corroborates the defendant's or the victim's story.

Stage directions read, "*There are dry leaves on the floor although the time is not fall*" (126). Fornes specifically denies the use of allegory; hence, the reader and spectator should also resist translating the elements of Fornes's set into easy symbols.[4] Fornes's leaves are more akin to Chekhov's seagull: they are images to be encountered, even sensually, but not interpreted. The leaves may be under the spectators' feet to keep the audience members aware of their physical presence *in* the scene, to remind them of their intrusion into this "private" space. Apparently, Julia is not the one uncomfortable here; though she hallucinates, Fornes indicates that "her behavior should not be the usual behavior attributed to a mad person. It should be rather still and luminous. There will be aspects of her hallucination that frighten her, but hallucinating itself does not" (126). In contrast, if the spectator is not actually frightened, she or he may be at least startled. While the stage is inhabited simultaneously by the actor and audience, who controls this stage space is tentative at best. The audience stands, confined to awkward shifting and probably an equally awkward silence, and surrounds a disabled "victim," while Julia, though flat on her back and apparently paralyzed, is "luminous" and vocal.

Given that Julia's speech describes her silencing, the audience is positioned as her silencers. At first Julia distinguishes between her tormentors and her spectators: "You don't think I'm going to argue with them do you," Julia asks rhetorically. "I repented. I told them exactly what they wanted to hear" (127). But, as she continues her monologue, her tormentors are in the room with her, sharing the spectators' space:

> *(Her head moves as if slapped.)*
> Don't hit me. Didn't I just say my prayer?
> *(A smaller slap.)*
> I believe it.
>
> (128)

To some extent Julia's posture is more important than the content of her speech. Her supine, covered, debilitated body is the central and powerful dramatic image of this scene, and the spectator's positioning underscores the primacy of that image. As the audience surrounds Julia, she is framed by *their* presence and by *their* gaze. The scene is about looking at Julia, to which her speech attests, by emphasizing "Woman" as an aesthetic and antiaesthetic object.[5] The audience's explicit positioning *within* this dramatic space reminds us not only to read Julia's literary text but also to read the text her body writes on the stage.

Fornes's use of the word *luminous* suggests that Julia's discourse is not madness but lucidity. Julia's experience is the inverse of Shakespeare's Desdemona. This is the woman's voice articulating a direct movement from physical abuse ("They clubbed me") to an effort at passive resistance ("I was good and quiet. I never dropped my smile") to self-loathing, explicitly gendered ("He said that women's entrails are heavier than anything on earth and to see a woman running creates a disparate and incongruous image in the mind. It's antiaesthetic. . . . He said that a woman's bottom should be in a cushion, otherwise it's revolting" [127]). By inverting Desdemona's experience, Julia has held off her death by her male tormentors. Julia's physical abuse causes her conversion, at least in word:

> The human being is of the masculine gender. . . . Everything on earth is for the human being, which is a man. . . . Woman is not a human being. She is:
> 1.—A mystery. 2.—Another species. 3.—As yet undefined. 4.—Unpredictable; therefore wicked and gentle and evil and good which is evil. . . .
> Man is not spiritually sexual, he therefore can enjoy sexuality. . . . Woman's

> spirit is sexual. . . . Their sexual feelings remain with them till they die. And
> they take those feelings with them to the afterlife where they corrupt the
> heavens, and they are sent to hell. (127)

Julia's ventriloquism answers in a male voice to Emma and Fefu's ruminations
about sex. She suggests that the result of seeing their vision through is the punishment she embodies—or the other side of the coin of their strength is her
weakness. Julia will use all the men's words put into her mouth, but the cost is
her woman's body. According to Julia, her acceptance of the physical abuse by
men is a means to survival. Fefu has made similar concessions; the black cat who
shits in her kitchen is the brother to Julia's hallucinations.

While Julia seems to embrace the male discourse, she also undermines it by
elevating it to that peculiar combination of lucidity and madness. By so thoroughly inhabiting the victimized woman's body, the woman beaten down by
man, she becomes somewhat two-dimensional, even while the scene's layout
emphasizes precisely her three-dimensionality; the spectator cannot avoid gaz-
ing at her body. In part Fefu's physical presence could not differ more from
Julia's. The contrast between these two women—one free to roam the stage, to
enter and exit, to elude the spectator's gaze at her will, and the other immobile
and dependent—can boil down to the physical use they will make of their bodies rather than to the philosophies they voice or the words they spew. In the
final account, however, Fefu's discourse is not dramatically different than Julia's.
Fefu also embraces male language ("I like being like a man" [117]) but believes
she does so within the realm of rational thought. Fefu believes her ventriloquism is not part of a disease; to Fefu her conversion (i.e., her use of male language and her embracing of a male perspective) is genuinely empowering; to
Julia her own conversion is about nothing more than staying alive. If Julia and
Fefu are on opposite ends of a philosophical spectrum, they are also coming
very close to closing the gap. And they are also opening that gap by inhabiting
their positions with such disparate physical presences.

Paula and Cecilia's exchange, "In the Kitchen," is comparatively simple.
Paula opens with a highly irreverent remark given the gravity of the scenes surrounding them. "I have it all figured out," she says. She seems at first to be discussing her contribution to their presentation, which is a ridiculous but potentially accurate account of love affair patterns. She has been working it out
mathematically: "3 months of love. 1 year saying: It's all right. This is just a pass-
ing disturbance. 1 year trying to understand what's wrong. 2 years knowing the
end had come" (129), and so on. Paula's calculations are preface to a discussion
of her terminated love affair with Cecilia. Her allegiance to formula (even if she

is joking) is consistent with the generally evasive content of her conversation with Cecilia. Their talk is not quite honest: "I've been meaning to call you," Cecilia says. "It doesn't matter. I know you're busy," Paula replies. Paula makes their inability to communicate explicit: "I speak and you don't understand my words" (130). The two women achieve closure only in the form of a superficial reconciliation. Yet the audience does *see* connection, intimacy, some kind of resolution, between the two lovers, even if their verbal trade belies this.

Each vignette in part 2 has shown women frustrated in their efforts to use language, but each has also shown women connecting with one another— physically, visibly, theatrically—in ways that have potential to be redemptive: Emma and Fefu embrace; Sue brings Julia a bowl of soup; each scene's pain or loneliness is mediated by the entrance of a woman who rejoins the woman or women in the scene to the other women in the house. In a sense throughout part 2 the women have all been preparing for part 3, for the rehearsal of their presentation, by rehearsing their own relationships. They have been exploring their characters in order to bring more to the final production.

Emma begins part 3 theatrically checking the light on her hand as she enters the room, and Cecilia walks in thoroughly engaged in formal speech. The women are building toward theater, but critically their presentation is mostly text, not spectacle, so the real theater within this drama is yet to come. Cecilia makes a subtle point about the work required of the spectator:

> We each have our own system of receiving information, placing it, respond-
> ing to it. That system can function with such a bias that it could take any sit-
> uation and translate it into one formula. That is, I think, the main reason for
> stupidity or even madness, not being able to tell the difference between
> things. . . . Like . . . this person is screaming at me. He's a bully. . . . Another
> person screams . . . and they have a good reason. (130–31)

Cecilia is concerned with the spectator's ability to identify motive and distinguish behavior and to respond accordingly. It is the spectator's burden rather than the actor's to unravel the truth. Part 3, then, begins with both the actors and the audience (re)entering the theater, so to speak. The spectator is reminded that text alone will not provide adequate access to understanding, even of theme or character. We are all brought back to the beginning.

Cecilia makes a critical connection between the spectator's role in the theater and the broader issue of the individual's role in community—an explicitly Fornesian concern. The spectator's task, like the citizen's, is to learn empathy: "We must be part of a community. . . . [E]ven the strongest will need a dozen, three, even one who sees, thinks and feels as they do." The theater, as a place in which to teach, has the responsibility of exposing its audience to the experience of others, and the spectator has the responsibility to accept and explore this exposure. "That is," Cecilia continues, "the concern of the educator—to teach how to be sensitive to the differences, in ourselves as well as outside ourselves. . . . Otherwise the unusual in us will perish" (131). Keyssar's "Drama and the Dialogic Imagination: *The Heidi Chronicles* and *Fefu and Her Friends*" (1991) is concerned precisely with this issue. Keyssar illustrates how *Fefu*'s success lies partly in

> presenting and urging the transformation of persons and our images of each other. This latter form of change requires not that we remove or have removed disguises that conceal us from our "true" selves, but that we imagine men and women in a continual process of becoming other. . . . [Drama] is the cultural space that most readily locates the viewer/reader outside, separate from an other. Drama . . . may lure us to see and shape others as identical to ourselves, but that is not what its best work is ever about . . . [rather, it is its] ability to enable us to acknowledge the otherness of others (93, 103).

When discussing her madness, Julia reprimands the audience members for their failure not only to see the other but also to experience and appreciate difference. Keyssar suggests that theater (and, by implication, any relationship between an "actor" and a "spectator") affords a rare opportunity to experience "multiple points-of-view" (99). Julia, whose madness often takes the shape of "becoming other" before our very eyes, in turn describes herself as the consummate victim of people's inability to empathize: "My hallucinations are madness, of course, but I wish I could be with others who hallucinate also. I would still know I am mad but I would not feel so isolated—Hallucinations are real, you know." If her hallucinations are Julia's real experience, and spectators try to see them with her, then their perceptions of reality will necessarily be broadened to include something of which they were not previously aware. Julia believes her hallucinations not only alienate her from others but elevate her as well; hence, to be empathic with her would be to receive a gift of sorts. Those who hallucinate can see more clearly. "If I were with other people who hallucinate they would say, 'Oh yeah. Sure. It's awful. Those dummies, they don't see anything'" (131). Julia is suggesting that the spectator take on the role of the hallucinatory—*see* that vividly, see the subtext to the text, see the person who is larger even than the sum of appearance and articulations, and, finally, see the woman through her hallucinations, which are "madness" but also "real."

Julia's character illustrates that the literary text is more stable (to the point

of being misleading) than the image's text. It is consistent, then, that in preparation for their presentation all of the women emphasize form over content, the
theater over the text, as they had done implicitly in parts 1 and 2. The text, or
general context, of the women's presentation is suspiciously de-emphasized by
its participants. Nearly each of them substitutes "blah blah blah" for the details
of their contributions. The theater's (their production on education included)
revelations will emerge at least as much from the visible as the audible. Hence,
as Fornes does often in her work, she moves the play in its final act to the realm
of metatheater, in order to reveal the real in the theatrical, the truth—behind,
beneath, of—the image. In *Fefu* the metatheatrical apex has two movements:
the rehearsal of their presentation and the final conflict between Fefu and Julia.

Emma's contribution to the presentation is featured above all else. As she
has directed, "dra-ma-tur-gia" (131) has drawn our attention to her, and now,
ironically, the length of her speech, rather than her physical presence, demands
our ears. Emma, like Fefu and Julia before her, is ventriloquizing, though she is
speaking a woman's words. Her text is taken from the prologue to *Educational
Dramatics* (1917) by Emma Sheridan Fry, and her topic is the individual's alienation from the self, caused by the rigidity of institutions. She describes humanity's sensory deprivation:

> Environment knocks at the gateway of the senses. A rain of summons beats
> upon us day and night. . . . We do not answer. Everything around us shouts
> against our deafness. . . . But we are deaf. The signals do not reach us.

Emma's speech is the literary equivalent of Julia's dramatization. Julia is the
individual who has lost the use of her senses. Emma's *us* answers to Julia's *they*
of part 2: "Society restricts us, school straight jackets us, civilization submerges
us, privation wrings us, luxury feather-beds us. . . . Thus we are taken by indif-
ference that is death" (132). It will become clear that her subject is specifically
women's alienation, even though she never uses the feminine pronoun. The
answer to "What are we?" is finally "Woman," waiting for her suitor: "We will
meet him. We will seize all, learn all, know all here, that we may fare further on
the great quest! . . . Let us awaken life dormant!" Emma makes a passionate plea
to women to seize control over their worlds. She puts their presentation
specifically into that context; these are women who, through theater, seek to
enter a world from which they have been barred. The effort must be creative:
"Let us then seek the laws governing real life forces, that coming into their
own, they may create, develop and reconstruct." And, she implies, their creation is under way. As Fefu says: "Now things don't need introduction. They
are happening" (133).

The women's theater balances the weight of Emma's speech, the literary text, with their own presences. They begin to act out their production for the audience, staging their roles, writing the text as they perform it. Paula says, "I offer the jewels of my wisdom and experience, which I will write down and memorize, otherwise I would just stand there and stammer and go blank," to which Emma responds, "I'll work with you on it." "However," Paula adds, "after our colleague Miss Emma Blake works with me on it. . . . My impulses will burst forth through a symphony of eloquence." Though they have an eye on the eventual product, their collaboration is making theater of the process.

Emma's literary peak demands a paralleled, or surpassing, theatrical peak, in order to both enhance and undermine its authority by sustaining its own ambiguous meaning (again, like Fefu's thought process in pt. 1). The water fight, a playfully theatrical gesture, prefaces the play's ultimate theatricality. Julia is of course barred from the games, as she is confined to her wheelchair, but she makes it clear that it is not only games she is removed from but all of living. She offers a prologue to her own death and dramatically attempts to justify herself as the human body that is always decaying, always vulnerable to death, which is the quintessence but not the exception to bodily abuses. "I feel we are constantly threatened by death, every second, every instant," she says. Life and death are indistinguishable to Julia; at least, life contains death: "Death is not anything. It's being lifeless." Julia asserts that she is saved from death by "guardians," which are the materialization of life in various forms, particularly the visual, which is no accident in the theater. To look at, to be a spectator, is encumbered with moral significance: "Our sight is a form [the guardians] take. That is why we take pleasure in seeing things, and we find some things beautiful." Even to Julia, then, using our senses is being alive, is what saves us from death. And using our senses is directly relevant to our treatment of others. From taking pleasure in seeing, Julia moves to looking at specific objects: "The sun is a guardian. . . . We enjoy looking at the sunlight when it comes through the window. . . . We, as people, are guardians to each other when we give love" (135), she concludes, asserting that it is in feeling *with* others that we keep ourselves alive.

That optimism notwithstanding, Julia dangerously believes that the guardians exist outside of herself; she has been so distanced from herself that she does not even own her senses. Thus, for Julia, she "will die . . . for no apparent reason" (135), though really because she will allow her own death to overtake her living. Julia's victimization is essentially consummated by her philosophy; she has given her own power away, delegated it to others (by implication, to men), and so assured her death. Fefu, then, is utterly exonerated of her final "crime" even before she and the audience see Julia walk. By the time we see

Julia walk into the living room for the sugar bowl (137), the gesture is theatrical punctuation to what we have already learned through her text: Julia does have power, but she has chosen not to use it.

Fornes and most of her characters sustain sympathy for Julia, despite her weakness. Julia's walking is narrated by Sue, whose voice functions as voice-over, heard from offstage. Though she is not talking about Julia, but about other women, the audience will likely hear her as if her subject is what we have just witnessed. Sue, then, reads Julia's condition as exhaustion that cannot, should not, be articulated or it will invite punishment. She and Emma describe women who did not wear their masks and were punished for it:

> Remember Susan Austin? She was very naive and when they asked her how she felt, she said she was nervous and she wasn't sleeping well. So she had to see a psychiatrist from then on. . . . Remember Julie Brooks? . . . At the end of the first semester they called her in because she had been out with 28 men and they thought that was awful. And the worst thing was that after that, she thought there was something wrong with her. . . . She was just very beautiful so all the boys wanted to go out with her. . . . She was really very innocent. (137)

Emma adds the story of Gloria Schuman, accused of plagiarism for a psychology paper and sent to a psychiatrist when she would not "admit" her crime. All three women are punished for their honesty as well as for their creative and intellectual efforts. Julia, Sue's voice-over implies, embodies the punishment for the cumulative "madness" inspired in all these women.

Paula removes the issue to an economic plane; the rich, she says, can afford to do something: "They should take the responsibility of everything that happens in the world. They are the only ones who can influence things. The poor don't have the power to change things." Coming on the heels of Sue and Emma's remarks, Paula implies that it is the responsibility of anyone in power to provoke change and, so, the responsibility of male authority in particular. Therefore, even though she knows "that's what we're doing. That's what Emma has been doing," she adds, "I guess I feel it's not enough" (139). Realistically, she implies, their women's theater can only do so much.

Within this very specific context, however, they have accomplished a great deal. Even at this particular moment they have provided Paula with the space in which she can be not only didactic and aggressive but also emotional. She sobs and, in turn, is kissed by Cecilia on the lips. And she is able to be loving and expressive: "I think highly of all of you" (139).

Fefu has been out on the lawn during this transaction—outside of the women's space, out in the men's space—and now seeks to bring that space in, or the women out, at least figuratively: "Have you been out?" she asks. "The sky is full of stars." Her reference may be directly to Emma's speech, as Emma had concluded: "Let us, boldly, seizing the star of our intent, lift it as the lantern of our necessity, and let it shine over the darkness of our compliance" (133). Emma's words serve as Fefu's inspiration for her almost honest confrontation of Julia. Julia denies she can walk, and Fefu accuses her of willing her disability: "You're nuts, and willingly so. . . . And you're contagious. I'm going mad too" (139). Fefu equates her dependency on Phillip with Julia's paralysis; both gestures, she asserts, are motivated by self-loathing, and both are simultaneously meant to justify that self-loathing. "Phillip can't stand me," she says. "He's left. His body is here but the rest is gone. . . . *(She holds Julia.)* I need him, Julia. . . . I try to leave him alone but I can't. I try to swallow my feelings but I can't. They choke me" (139–40). Fefu is never specific about either what she wants from Phillip or even what she needs. It is all about process for Fefu, rather than product; it is the fruitless searching that causes her so much pain, though it is the searching, too, that distinguishes her. Fefu recognizes that Julia is victim to the same fears and has therefore embraced the pain, even become the pain, in order to face no longer the terrible frustrations of unmet needs. Julia has elected the "rest" that Fefu both wants and fears: "I want to rest, Julia. How does a person rest. I want to put my mind at rest. I am frightened and I am overbearing—I look into your eyes and I know what you see." But then she adds, "I'm not giving in" (140). If what Julia sees in Fefu is a woman who naively insists on fighting a futile battle to the end, Fefu sees in Julia a woman who naively believes her battles are fought for her and are either won or lost. Fefu may be "overbearing"—her presence may be theatrical and intrusive—but the alternative is the kind of invisibility that threatens Julia.

Literarily speaking, the final theatrical moment of the drama is essentially after the fact, the exclamation point to a sentence that has already punctuated itself through its content. Julia has been living a death in life, and Fefu's "shooting" her only dramatizes that fact. Julia has made clear that death is her own choice, but, by insisting that the agents of her death are outside of her, she has essentially coerced Fefu into that role. Fornes's metatheatricality obscures any unraveling of agency: Fefu shoots a rabbit, not Julia, though Julia has blood on her forehead at the moment of her death—but Fefu *is* the one holding the gun.[6] Julia has emerged as the victim of Fefu and Phillip's sport, but that still does not answer precisely what she is a victim to. To Fefu's playing a man's role, the role of the hunter, to Phillip's ultimate control as the loader of the gun, to the reverberations of power plays between women and men, between women and women?

Metatheatrically, the playwright is responsible. Fornes has directed Fefu to act in a manner that contrasts with Julia's acting, to act "well," in contrast to Julia's acting "poorly." Julia has given up her right to act, to be an agent, so Fefu has been forced to take on the entire burden of the actor's role. It remains difficult, however, to say whether Fefu's final theatrical gesture is productive or destructive. The language of the drama has rendered that question moot: Julia has articulated her own death.[7] Finally, the play's ultimate moment is not about language but about theater. In a sense, as long as Julia has been allowed to inhabit this stage space, she has done damage to the female subject on the stage, perpetuated the image of woman as victim and as an object of scrutiny, confined to madness. Fefu's violence, then, might provide space for a different kind of female subject, one not reduced to the object Julia was reduced to, one not bonded to male discourse.

Despite the potential productivity of Fefu's violence, Fornes's play by no means offers Fefu's solution as entirely palatable. Fefu closes no gaps and offers up no new choices for women by "murdering" Julia. Her own dilemma partic- ularly has not been resolved. To the contrary, killing a woman dramatizes the fear that Fefu has been articulating since part 1; it is a gesture that involves silencing, dishonesty, and the thwarting of self-knowledge. But what Fefu has accomplished is genuine agency of some sort; her physical presence entirely controls the spectacle of these stage events, and, even by reinforcing Julia's role as object, Fefu is acting out the role of subject. To act has been Fefu's triumph.

Throughout *Fefu and Her Friends* the theatrical term *spectacle* has been sub- ject to piercing scrutiny, even redefinition. Julia has been little more than spec- tacle; Fornes has made the spectator focus on the women's relationships as spec- tacle by compelling perambulations around their scenes; and the conflict between Fefu and Julia culminates in the pure spectacle of a shotgun blast and spouting blood. Theater, and lyrical theater particularly, she implies, is entirely spectacle; its significance comes from its being looked at. To distinguish, then, between spectacle and theme or character, for example, is artificial. The entire drama is part of the spectacle. The subject is also an object. By choosing to sit still, Julia gives in to this threat; by laudably refusing to sit still, Fefu perpetuates these exact dangers. To overcome being reduced from agent to spectacle endures as the ultimate trial for women on Fornes's stages.

Mud

The triangular relationship between two men and one woman in *Mud* (1983) recalls the eccentric marriage of He, She, and 3 from *The Successful Life of 3* nearly two decades earlier. As He, She, and 3 were bound to their theatrical event—happily enough in the end—*Mud*'s characters are more ominously bound to their stage. As in Samuel Beckett's *Endgame,* the players are snared in this claustrophobic stage space, and eventually the spectator also comes to doubt whether there is, in fact, any place else to go. That claustrophobia is echoed within the relationships between characters. There is no room for growth; any change will be chaotically disruptive.

The play represents the shifts in power of three characters—Henry, who is literate; Mae, who is attempting to learn; and Lloyd, who hovers between the two—shifts that replace a more linear plot. We see the characters enact their power struggles in highly theatrical vignettes characterized by frozen poses and self-conscious, often melodramatic speech. While not plot driven, this play, like so many of Fornes's others, moves toward a climax, though, typically, not a moment of recognition for the characters or even the spectators. The conclusion *shows* that the first image's prophecy comes true: no productive power can be gained when the players so obstinately avoid genuine knowledge.

As in *Fefu and Her Friends,* Mae's efforts to increase her own agency threaten the integrity of the other actors on the stage. Mae, Lloyd, and Henry are rigidly characterized specifically in order to emphasize character as determined by theatrical above psychological or literary context. As a lyrical enterprise, character in this drama is defined through the theater, through spectacle, through encounters, against the set. This is not about a woman coming to consciousness but, rather, about characters struggling to inhabit the stage. Though Fornes offers a story of sorts—Henry moves into Mae and Lloyd's home and relationship, eventually unsettling both and causing all three characters' connections to undergo activity, if not actual change—the play's movement more accurately should be described formally: above all else, these characters are props for one another.

Relying on Henry and Lloyd as a stable foundation, Mae attempts to achieve agency through language, the one "prop" on the stage whose control she should not have to share with Henry and Lloyd. Though she shares this theatrical space with these apparently immovable men, Mae's search for her self, for subjectivity, is an inward search characterized mostly by her efforts to use language to express her sense of self *to* herself. In the failure of those efforts Fornes suggests that what foils Mae is in part the direction of her search; Mae's developing use of language does not forge any connection with the world around her, does not recognize a fundamental purpose of language to communicate with one's community, to enable one to extend outward rather than confining one to the prison of one's self. There is no self without the expression of that self to others, Fornes insists, or without receivers for that expression. In the last act of the play Mae physically tries to move outward, but her efforts are futile, because she has not learned to use language as a bridge; hence, that movement is not supported by the men she wants to move away from.

Some critics would like to see in the play the emergence through Mae of a female subject; I see the implosion of a female subject.[1] That the kitchen, traditionally the woman's space, is centered here has drawn feminist commentary,[2] and Mae might well be considered the protagonist (if we use the phrase loosely). Mae will also draw the spectator's attention precisely because of her physical difference from the other two characters as well as through Fornes's staging of her, even the predominance of her role as speaker. Most important, as the victim of the most severe violence in a play about violence, Mae is at the very least the central object here, if not the central subject. But, if the play ends on Mae's realization of her self, or some aspect of her self, it also ends simultaneously with her death, with the utter and complete loss of the self. To celebrate her achieving subjectivity, then, is romantic at best.

The set belies Mae's inevitable failure to achieve autonomy. There will be no escaping the world of this play, in which the centripetal illusion of the scene, the presence of all props within the stage space from the onset, and the literal, imagistic depiction of the play's central metaphor, mud, make it unnecessary to look beyond the stage for meaning. The drama uses mud as a significant presence in its own right, not just symbol but context. The mud's comparable presence to the kitchen's presence (the promontory is "five feet high and covers the same periphery as the room" [15]) evokes a visual balance (if not only a symbolic balance) between the world these characters inhabit and the world that threatens them. As far as the eye can see—and that may be what matters most in the theater—the mud is a base for Mae's kitchen: context *and* subtext. Even if no action transpires there, the spectator will see colors reflected and remember to look there when Mae evokes mud as metaphor, which she does frequently. Though spectators cannot see into the mud as they can see into the kitchen, the mud will seem a threatening and potentially consuming shadow of the kitchen. Its weight as both image and metaphor will always be felt. The mud will always ground even Mae's loftiest poetry, as it pulls the blue sky down into the bulk of the stage. What the spectators see will always counter what the characters would like us to see, even the appearance of change within their relationships and personal lives.

The set for Fornes's *Mud* seems to funnel inward, from the expansive blue background, which represents the sky, to the red "earth promontory" of mud on which Mae's kitchen sits to the centered white of "wood . . . the color and texture of bone that has dried in the sun" (15). White will also prove to be the color of Lloyd's diseased tongue, and we may suppose it is a white light that Mae dies into at the play's end. In fact, in act 1, scene 1, Mae imagines the perfect death as swathed in whiteness. Whiteness will be her reward for self-education: "I am going to die in a hospital," she tells Lloyd. "In white sheets. . . . Clean feet. Injections. . . . I'm going to die clean. I'm going to school and I'm learning things" (19). Mae reserves blue for her fantasy of Lloyd's death: "You'll die like a pig in the mud," she insists. "Your skin will bloat. . . . Then, it will get blue like rotten meat and it will bloat even more" (19). In the context of the world of this play—a world finally colorful, in which the sky's blue will heighten the earth's red by comparison—Mae desires a pure and colorless death, condemning Lloyd to a colorful death for punishment.

As Mae articulates it, she would like her death to be an inward movement, mimicking the set's movement toward whiteness, a dying into herself. It is not surprising that Mae does not imagine death as a potentially expansive movement (its brightness notwithstanding), given that her world is no larger than the kitchen she inhabits with Lloyd and Henry, fellows in poverty and ignorance. And, indeed, Mae's death in the play's final scene is an implosion, despite the explosive sounds of Lloyd's gun shots. Her death at the play's end follows inevitably from Mae's solitary life; annihilating violence unavoidably erupts when Mae seeks escape from so obdurate an environment. These characters are ruled by poverty and ignorance, and, thematically, the play is essentially a theatricalization of the violence that poverty and ignorance can do to the spirit, mind, and body. None of the characters is spared that fury, and none are not guilty of perpetuating it.

In turn *Mud* begins and ends with violence. The first scene depicts brutality verbally and emotionally and needs only continued theatricalization to confirm its power. That the violence will turn physical is essentially a foregone conclusion; violence to the spirit (synonymous with the intellect for both Fornes and Mae) is a kind of physical violence. Throughout the drama the futility of discourse is paralleled by the uselessness of physical violence; similarly, the violence of characters' language is increasingly paralleled by violent physical behavior. The mutual development along these lines prevents any *real* development, miring the characters in a circular process. The only real change occurs at the drama's end, or even just after the curtain falls, with the loss of one point in this triangle of characters. Mae's death in and of itself is only an image that literalizes the death-in-life that has been her truth. Fornes emphasizes context in this play in order to make a broad political statement about the powerlessness of the individual against the power of the institutions the individual inhabits. Whether it is the character within the framework of the theatrical event or the woman in her kitchen where two men go to great pains to control her, the outcome is the same. Without the ability to disrupt the context, Mae is confined to the roles she already plays.

In *Mud*'s first scene Mae stands while Lloyd sits, a posture the audience will see both physically and dramatically overturned. Mae uses language carefully. When Lloyd asks what Mae does at school, she tries to ascertain whether he really cares. When it becomes clear to her that he cares only for the blow to his ego, rather than the boon to her own, she gets angry. Lloyd begins the verbal abuse: "Don't talk back to me," he says. "I'll kick your ass." Mae responds: "Fuck you, Lloyd. I'm telling you about arithmetic and you talk to me like that?" Mae may be uneducated and not all that eloquent at this point, but she can already use language to express herself succinctly.[3] Mae verbally wins the argument, couched in terms of sex as commodity, by getting the last word. "I don't even want to fuck you," Lloyd says, to which Mae responds: "You can't, that's why. You can't get it up" (17). But Lloyd wins the argument visually. When it is clear that language will be an inadequate weapon for him, he shifts to the sure power of physicality. He attempts to soothe the pain of his insecurity by trying to dominate Mae sexually. He holds her hand on his crotch.

For Fornes, however, this does not make Mae the obvious victim. Her aspirations to education alone threaten violence to this scene; there is no place for her educated self in the space of this particular dramatic world. And, though

Lloyd ends up holding the gun, as it were (the scene ends with the ax in Lloyd's grasp), Fornes does not deny him her sympathy. When Mae threatens Lloyd with the life of solitude, even literal hunger, that would ensue from her abandonment of him, he admits that he "did it to Betsy" (20), a pig from the yard outside their home. He counters what he receives as Mae's violent threat with the image of some offstage violence (violence that is inherently threatening to Mae as well—i.e., she can be replaced too). But Lloyd wants his audience to believe, with him, that the experience of having sex with Betsy was neither violent nor ugly. "It didn't hurt," he insists and even adds: "She's nice. She lets me eat her food" (20). Not unlike Mae, Lloyd acknowledges the power of language by trying to evoke, through language, an image whose lack of violence can counter the subtext of violence. As Mae does, he tries to use language as a lens through which the images of reality can be altered. Like Mae's fantasy about her clean death, Lloyd's fantasy tries to clean up his life (provocatively, Mae wonders, "Did you get clean before you did it?" worrying about Betsy's hygienic safety rather than Lloyd's). But for both characters the imagistic context conspires against them; they cannot obliterate the violence already evoked. Mae cannot make clean, through language, what is dirty, what sits on a pile of mud, as Lloyd cannot make clean the image of his "doing it" to a pig.

The gaps between what Mae and Lloyd try to evoke through language and the actual stage events underscore the authority of what the spectator *sees*. Between tableaux the spectator watches the actors (possibly out of character but not necessarily) change the set. The theatrical self-consciousness of that maneuver reminds the spectators that the entire dramatic world of this play is contained in the space we see. Mae takes a prop (a brown paper bag from the mantelpiece) from the onstage set then plays as if she got it offstage. As Lloyd's description of sex with Betsy gives the act qualities it could not have had (he anthropomorphizes the pig and renders quiet and lovely what could not have been), Mae's between-scene gesture implies that we need not acknowledge anything beyond this stage space as relevant to the events herein. The stage's reality is carefully constructed as utterly true even in its self-containment and utterly irrelevant to offstage reality. It follows, however ironically, that Lloyd's mating with Betsy, as described by Lloyd, is the truth of that event as he needs to know it; the tableau he conjures verbally is the truth for him. Whatever else the spectator thinks he or she knows, at this stage in the drama the power of language cannot be minimized, even if its ultimate power is suspect, given the visual context of the play.

In fact, the ability to use language can be precisely what centers any particular character in this drama. While Mae carefully places herself center stage at the start of act 1, scene 2, replacing the spectator's attention from Lloyd at the end of act 1, scene 1, ax in hand, she is eventually replaced by Henry. Not only is the spectator's physical focus shifted but his or her aural focus as well. Henry becomes the text's mouthpiece, the authority, as he reads from the pamphlet what Mae cannot read. Henry makes Lloyd's illness especially vivid:

> Febrile illness, back pains, perineal pain, irritative voiding, aching of the perineum, sexual pain, sexual impotency, painful ejaculation, and intermittent disureah, or bloody ejaculation. (22)

The dramatic world of *Mud* is not extending out into the space beyond the stage—not even to the clinic from which the pamphlet presumably came, since we know it came from the set—but into the invisible verbal space within the stage, even within the characters themselves. Ominously, language comes to occupy, or so it seems, its own space, separate from the world the spectator can see and yet portentously the key to making sense of that world. The spectator, though not the characters, is being taught to be especially distrustful of language.

Act 1, scene 2, ends with more verbal deception, to which both the characters and audience are subject. From the careful, terrible delineation of the symptoms of Lloyd's disease, the image shifts to Mae's offering dinner to Henry. Lingering is the image of Lloyd's sickly white tongue or even the image Mae has evoked of Lloyd digging his own grave: "You better dig your own grave while you can, Lloyd," Mae says. "I told him to find a spot and dig it. It takes a strong person to dig that deep. I can't do it. I wouldn't, even if I could" (23), Mae says, shifting from the adage to the image. But, with Mae's offer of dinner to Henry, she brings the spectator's attention back to the stage, reminding us of the context for anything verbally evoked. Verbally evoked images matter only in the context of the theatrical event we witness.

Mae's most important insight into the nature of the theater lies in her apparent understanding of the theater as a forum for the representation of the image and text *in process*. She recognizes, then, the space in which she might alter her self and her story. In act 1, scene 3, Mae seduces Henry in a scene with metatheatrical reverberations (let alone political reverberations; Mae plays a typically "masculine" role). Mae attempts to alter context actively through text. She manipulates the manuscript like a playwright: to her assertion that she wants Henry to live with her, he responds, "To live here?"; to her assertion "I want your mind," he responds, "My mind?" Moreover, she manages to manipulate the text by converting their general conversation about the value of objects (their lack of inherent value, their need for context) to the value of the individual: "Some people make you feel that you have something inside you. . . . What I'm saying, Henry, is that I want you" (24). Simultaneously, she moves more and more closely toward him, completing the movement with two kisses. Mae has both put words in another's mouth, the playwright's role, and staged the physical progress of their relationship, the director's role. But, forebodingly, Mae lacks a comprehension of the minds of her characters; she is essentially directing with her eyes closed, with both an inadequate sense of the nature of their present in this theatrical world and the possibilities for the future.

Though Mae may not be entirely aware of context, Fornes ensures her audience's focus there by keeping the art foregrounded. At the end of each scene *"a freeze is indicated. These freezes will last eight seconds which will create the effect of a still photograph"* (16). On the one hand, each scene reaches a visual climax, forcing the spectator to concentrate on the image that most endures from the scene's progress, the image that essentially outlasts the text, giving that image primacy over the text.[4] But the stills also draw attention to their own artificiality. The scene's process is rudely interrupted by the revelation of the art behind it. The verity of both the text and the image are undermined. Both are put into quotation marks, referring the spectator to the subtext of the accumulation of both text and image, that is, to the *inclusive* theatrical text.[5]

Mae's commitment to the power of language is emphasized in the next few scenes, but, while she is attentive to its strengths in terms of what it can do for her, she neglects to make the leap toward what it can do for others or for her relationships with others. In one scene Mae's speech and Lloyd's reactive pantomime illustrate the consequences of both Mae's literal and literary actions. Mae is distinguished as powerful *through* language. She narrates their immediate future: "Henry is going to stay here with us. . . . Henry's going to sleep in the bedroom. . . . You can sleep here.—Get papers from the shed and lay them on the floor" (25). Mae shapes the future as she speaks. Lloyd, on the other hand, is powerless in the context of this particular scene, specifically because of his lack of language. The text reads, *"He is distraught. He sits on the chair on the left and cries. He puts his head on the table and freezes"* (25).

The next scene suggests that Mae's vigor comes not only from her use of language in speech but also in her more general use of language as poet, reader, writer, actor, and critic. First, she directs Henry to offer grace for their meal, then she practices a kind of reader-response: "I feel grace in my heart," she says. "I feel fresh inside as if a breeze had just gone through my heart." She makes use of the art, empowering herself through the medium of her sensual response. But, unapologetically, she seeks little in the way of interpretation or intellectual understanding. Mae continues: "I don't retain the words. . . . I don't remember the things I learn too well. . . . But I rejoice with the knowledge that I get" (26). Knowledge, for Mae, is essence rather than substance. As is so often true for Fornes's heroines, meaning is never something you just hold in your hand but, rather, what you do with it once it is there. Mae asks Henry to repeat grace (to underscore the rhyme, as it were) and responds emotionally again, even more intensely with tears and perfect empathy. "I am a hungry soul," she answers to Henry's "For [God] satisfies the longing soul, and fills the hungry soul with goodness." "I am a longing soul," Mae adds. "It satisfies me to hear words that speak so lovingly to my soul." Mae forces the text to speak directly to her; by reiteration she even makes it her own text. And, finally, Mae guarantees herself the last word in this scene with a comment that borders on non sequitur, giving her even more control over the direction of discourse. Somewhat abruptly, she concludes: "Don't be afraid to eat from our dishes, Henry. They are clean" (27). On the one hand, the spectators are thrust back to the visual image, essentially instructed to stop listening to text and to remember to consider the image before them. In this case the redirecting of attention will be ominous in retrospect; what the spectators *see* is three people at a table; what they *hear* is Mae's inability to make the leap from an awareness that language enables her to express herself to using language to communicate with others. But the spectators are also returned to the very real physical context of the scene, which helps to ground Mae's spirituality. She compels not only Henry and Lloyd's respect and attention but the respect and attention of her more general spectator as well.

The next scene provides an actual text to support Mae's self-characterization. Text is specifically foregrounded as Mae reads from her book while Lloyd listens silently. Mae's "inspired" reading describes the purely sensory starfish: functional ("They keep the water clean"), sensitive ("A starfish's eye cannot see. But they can tell if it is night or day"), and mysterious ("no one really knows" how long they live). The spectator should already know that Mae will empathize with what she reads here—she might do so even if the description of the starfish were not so apt, simply because it is her own voice reading aloud— but the text that Mae reads is especially meaningful as an indication of Mae's sense of herself as worthy of textual description and even of herself as the conjurer of such an image. Mae briefly perceives of herself as a text, and, even though she is not the author of this particular document, she perceives herself as authoritative, as capable of poetic articulation.

Before either Mae or her spectators can become too confident of Mae's command, the visual tableau replaces the text with a single and succinct gesture.

Stage directions read: *"Lloyd slaps the book off the table. Mae slaps Lloyd. They freeze"* (27). The final and enduring image of this scene, then, is not only of Mae's desperate desire for the authority of the artist, for access to both knowledge and feeling, but of the conflict between herself and Lloyd that her desire provokes. The text and image work together to describe the insecurity, poverty (of material, of spirit), and ignorance that thwart any progress in this drama. Inexorably, the truth emerges that the text *cannot* advance as long as the image has this much potency.

Even those images that the audience is exposed to between scenes have the power to affect readings of both text and image. Responsibility for props between scenes is delegated differently than during scenes; Lloyd also handles the book, for example. And the characters' maneuvers between scenes are not strictly functional; that is, both Mae and Lloyd move the book between act 1's scenes 6 and 7. The spectator's response to Lloyd must be affected by his at least dual role. Henry's opening line in act 1, scene 7, instructs the spectator to be attentive to the impact of Lloyd's resulting elusiveness. He asks Mae, "What is Lloyd to you?" which is what the image has also just asked of the spectator (even of Mae, for that matter). The tableau insists that character is subject to context, to the context of the enacted drama as well as to the ineffable context of those more elaborate images and emotions that are not, cannot be, staged.

Mae suggests that her relationship with Lloyd has been altered specifically because of the new context her relationship with Henry provides. She describes her alliance with Lloyd to Henry as "like animals who grow up together and mate," but she says that has changed since Henry has moved in: "I could not be his mate again, not while you are here. I am not an animal. I care about things, Henry, I do" (28). She claims that both her relationship with Lloyd and her self-definition have been redefined within the new format of these broader relationships.

What Mae urges through her words, however, is inconsistent with the image she provides, both linguistically and visually. The honesty and careful description of her relationship with Lloyd—her use of detail particularly—finally seem to celebrate that relationship. She rehearses their history together, their childhood, her father's bringing Lloyd home, and then her father's death, which left she and Lloyd a family of sorts in their own right. "I don't know what we are," she insists. "We are related but I don't know what to call it." Language, she claims, fails her, though she has so successfully evoked the quality of her relationship with Lloyd. "Lloyd is good, Henry," she adds. And, more important: "And this is his home" (28). Context is apparently not as much altered as she would like to believe.

Presumably, on some level Mae is conscious of the context's tenacity. She turns to Henry and contradicts her assertion that she is "not an animal." "I don't want to live like a dog," she insists, disclosing her fear that she lives precisely that way. And Mae is down on her knees, just like a dog, begging Henry neither to leave nor to be too disgusted with her and Lloyd. This image of Mae contrasts so severely with the image of the powerful woman Mae has tried, often successfully, to evoke. Ironically, despite her intentions, in this scene Mae has strengthened the spectator's perception of the positive aspects of her relationship with Lloyd—something like respect and care—while undermining her own assertions about the strengths of her relationship with Henry. By comparison, the latter relationship is far too abstract, too intellectual. *That* relationship is the one that eludes words and is best described by image.

Scenes 8 and 9 end act 1 with images that illustrate not the shortcomings of Mae and Lloyd's relationship but the gaps in Mae and Henry's. Henry's gift to Mae of lipstick and a mirror in scene 8 essentially leave her speechless: "Lipstick. . . . A mirror. . . . Oh, Henry" (29), Mae says. The text has nothing to add to the scene's absurdity; Mae has no intelligible response. What does she need with lipstick?[6] And, in order to ensure that the spectator will be aware of this absurdity, the final scene of act 1 shows Mae actively back to her textbook; in fact, the lipstick scene is framed by Mae's reading and writing in its juxtaposing scenes.

Finally, the inner text of the first act's final scene—the text within the text—severs Mae from the drama's movement. The absurd objectification of Mae that Henry's gift begins is perpetuated when Henry and Lloyd become the central actors. Mae is reduced to setting, to the stage for Henry and Lloyd's struggle, imaged in the shell of a hermit crab. Mae reads from her textbook the description of a hermit crab's territorial demands: "Often he tries several shells before he finds the one that fits. Sometimes he wants the shell of another hermit crab and then there is a fight" (29). None of these characters are able to work this observation into a parable, but each can certainly recognize its aptness, as it leaves them speechless. All three exchange looks, and the scene ends with the men eyeing each other, with Mae, figuratively at least, now outside of both the text and the image.

As act 1 ends with all eyes on the men, act 2 begins as the men's drama, prophesying Mae's further demise. Act 2, scene 10, involves only Henry and Lloyd, cast in the somewhat conventional roles of father and son, or authority and subject, roles that seem to materialize inevitably from the context. Lloyd is reduced to a stuttering child desperately seeking help: "They gave me *this*," Lloyd says, to which Henry responds, "That's the prescription for your medicine," and Lloyd again, apparently retarded, "They said I should buy *this*" (30). While Henry may have originally seemed virtuous, by way of what Mae wanted him to be, and Lloyd villainous, the reversal process is under way. Lloyd is becoming an increasingly sympathetic character, particularly in contrast to Henry, who is didactic and cruel, even while Lloyd is so obviously fragile. Act 2 begins, then, by focusing on Lloyd as this drama's most obvious victim, rather than Mae. When Mae is reinvolved in the drama, she is efficient and productive, in strong contrast to both the men. But, ironically, for all her activity Mae controls the drama less at this point than she has at any other. Though she plays a variety of roles considerably more complicated than those of Lloyd and Henry, each of those roles is in service to the men. She doctors Lloyd by physically helping him to swallow his pills, holding his head back and forcing the pills down his throat. And she acts as arbitrator in Lloyd and Henry's argument over Lloyd's theft of Henry's money for his medicine. Mae speaks to both of the men, for both of them, further displacing the conflict onto them and away from herself. She is both indirectly the commodity they are bargaining for and the one doing the bargaining, essentially erasing herself. Forced into the various roles designed to accommodate the men—nurse, caretaker, voice of emotion, voice of reason—the play's emphasis shifts from Mae as agent to Mae as medium. She is no longer the artist; Mae provides the stage on which the men can enact *their* drama.

As these characters would have it, plot progress is ultimately responsible for the roles they play. In act 2, scene 12, Lloyd has his strength back, obviously inspired by Henry's loss of strength (due to an offstage fall). Lloyd and Henry's relationship has become symbiotic, as these two crabs vie for the same shell, bargaining with the same money, whose right to possession is dubious at best—it might even be Mae's money. Mae becomes defeatist, giving over the drama to Lloyd. As Mae reasons it, Lloyd might as well kill Henry, since "he can't talk straight anymore" (34). All of her power, as she saw it, or her potential for power, was in the possibility of intellectual discourse with Henry. Now that the struggle has been funneled into a physical struggle between the men, she assumes she no longer has a place in their drama.

Mae is still more of an agent than she acknowledges. She still has the authority to insist that she and Lloyd will take care of Henry in his infirmity. By way of that insistence Mae exercises her continued control over Lloyd; in fact, the spectator sees much more of Lloyd's physical caretaking of Henry than of Mae's. Act 2, scene 13, finds Lloyd feeding Henry, now literally. Typically Fornesian, however, Mae's agency cannot be independent of either Lloyd or Henry's agency. Who has the most power on this stage is highly ambiguous at this point. As long as Lloyd and Mae will respond to Henry's needs, he becomes increasingly powerful even while appearing at least physically powerless. Insofar as a character's boundaries are determined by the other characters—that is, the extent to which character is defined against other characters—Mae and Lloyd's responsiveness to Henry undermines their autonomy. Though the characters may see their actions as determined by plot, Fornes suggests that they are more elaborately determined by the other characters.

Again, Mae claims to believe that her recourse is what she can either give or withhold through speech: "Kill him if you want.—He can't talk straight anymore" (34). Mae blames Henry's muteness for her modified desires. But one wonders what Mae ever got from Henry. While she has alluded to intelligent conversation between them, the spectator has no evidence; we have heard Mae's intelligence, but the only evidence of Henry's intelligence is his ability to read or, possibly, Mae's faith in him. As far as the spectator is concerned, nothing has changed about Mae's relationship with Henry, except her perceptions. Mae's desire for Henry—specifically, for his supposed intelligence—has had a command over her all along that has enabled her to avoid the true vacuousness of their relationship, even her vacuous self, and to see instead what she has wanted to see. Mae's self-definition could not have been more enmeshed in her desire for another or, more specifically, in her efforts to make another into what she herself wanted to be. When she knows for certain that her desire will not be satisfied, she can no longer sustain the illusion of an intelligent and valuable relationship between herself and Henry.

Essentially, the entire conflict dramatized in *Mud* has been an illusion. Events have been predetermined by the inadequate power of language and the inevitable power of context. All that has remained undetermined was whether any character would change sufficiently to alter the chain of events—or whether characters would make room for such changes in one another. The metamorphoses that Lloyd and Henry *seem* to go through do not alter the context, because of their symbiosis: one of them is always a burden for Mae and always will be. The interconnectedness of the lives of these characters, the extent to which they do not exist outside of one another—cannot exist, theatrically speaking—allows no space for such change in characterization. Their theatrical space is too small and constricted. Mae will never get either enough power or pleasure from her capacities, because those capacities will never be happily met by Lloyd and Henry. If language has a resilience or beauty in this play, even if we consider it the language of the illiterate and inarticulate, the tragedy here is that even that cannot save these characters, bound as they are to the theater they inhabit. Toby Zinman labels *Mud* absurdist theater in part because, "linguistically, it demonstrates simultaneously both the inadequacy and the dazzling beauty of words" (218). What is most bleak, then, is how little that beauty counts. When Lloyd tries to teach himself to read, an act that might satisfy Mae enormously, she knows, instead, the irrelevance of that gesture. For Mae Lloyd's trying to learn to read is the same kind of ridiculing mimicry of her as Henry's aping and laughing at Lloyd's efforts at pronunciation. The gesture only reveals to Mae the context they are mired in; both of their efforts are a joke.

That Mae lacks empathy for Lloyd is not entirely her fault. In this particular dramatic world, so void of both empathy and sympathy for Mae, she especially cannot take pleasure in Lloyd's efforts at self-education. He had ridiculed those efforts of hers and, moreover, indirectly would deny Mae what would have been her own, what might have distinguished her. But Mae is responsible here for thwarting change in both hers and Lloyd's plot and their theatrical context. She is suppressing Lloyd's character development and, hence, suppressing her own. Not unlike Julia in *Fefu and Her Friends,* Mae has bowed to context and figured her own death-in-life.

The increasingly violent subtext—the violence that has been partially realized in Lloyd's illness, Henry's crippling, and Mae's objectification—continues to beg its theatrical equivalent, as did the conflict between Julia and Fefu in *Fefu*. Act 2, scene 15, a literally climactic scene (Henry masturbates to orgasm), is pivotal to the mounting violence. In a plea for Mae's love Henry masturbates in front of her, to her as it were, and in context, making a particularly selfish kind of love. Henry endeavors to compel a response from Mae, but he clearly does not know where to aim. He blames Mae for their deteriorating relationship: "You think a cripple has no feelings" (37), he says, typically underestimating Mae's intelligence. In fact, she knows fully well that he has no feelings in the phrase's clichéd sense; that is, he has no feelings for others, including herself. Henry does provoke a response from Mae but, presumably, the inverse of what he had anticipated. When he has an orgasm, Mae also collapses (onto a chair), but there is nothing sympathetic about her response. Rather, she appears to be responding to the inherent violence of his selfish gesture (when he might have made a sexual gesture that actually reached out to Mae, a gesture *for* her), the violence that his selfish desire does to her.

Mae is also guilty of a dangerous kind of masturbation. Her seduction of Henry was entirely self-serving; she had nothing to offer him. In this sense Henry's masturbating, like Lloyd's before him, dramatizes certain truths about *all* of their conditions. Mae has tried to use language and poetry for her pleasure alone. Hence, that language fails Mae is inevitable, given the extent to which she uses it only self-reflexively, the extent to which she does not make enough effort to use it for communication with others. For all the characters the danger lies in the divestment of meaning in words. At the close of act 2, scene 16, both men shout "I love you" to Mae, which could not be a greater waste of words.

What is finally so menacing about Mae, Lloyd, and Henry's mutual inarticulateness is the power that it gives to the drama, to the theatrical image. Without adequate language they cannot reshape either the images of their surrounding world or their own images. Mud, though present all along, reasserts itself toward the end of the drama as a place in which Mae is especially swamped. Between scenes 15 and 16 Lloyd enacts a particular kindness: he helps Henry back up onto a chair and closes his fly. That kindness, portrayed in the shadow between scenes, circumscribes Mae's violence of act 2, scene 16. When she finds her money in Henry's pocket, she threatens to choke him with his tie and concludes, "You're a pig, Henry" (38). Though Mae suggests the mud is Henry's, what is most striking here is that Mae has been unable to escape the mud, despite her apparently profound efforts.

While the unspoken pact between the men to take care of each other seems to make Mae the villain, even to invest her with the greatest powers of agency, the shift of focus back onto Mae at a point where the violence demands its most theatrical realization simultaneously locates her as the most likely victim. The penultimate scene of the drama is strikingly unfinished, both verbally and imagistically. The obvious inadequacies, even falseness, of the men's demonstrations of love reverberate and require correction, and the mounting violence demands an ultimate victim. The last scene begins with Mae on the brink of escape, though that theatrical possibility is undermined by the dramatic facts of her bondage. Mae is still trying to talk her way out: "I work too hard and the two of you keep sucking my blood. I'm going to look for a better place to be. Just a place where the two of you are not sucking my blood" (39). She carefully articulates (and accentuates with repetition) her awareness that she has no self in the context of this particular stage event, has no self in the presence of these two other dramatically demanding characters.

The violence that will finally annihilate Mae takes place offstage—it does not matter; she is already lost. The men narrate Lloyd's murder of Mae with Henry's "plaintive" and "incoherent" sounds and both of their repeated shouting of her name. Her name is, in fact, briefly the only intelligible text, and that text says very little. It seems to give Lloyd a target, something to aim at, more than anything else. Offstage Lloyd shoots Mae twice, even though the silence following the first shot suggests a successful hit. When Lloyd carries Mae back onto the stage, "drenched in blood and unconscious," we are treated to more irrelevant commentary. Lloyd concludes, "She's not leaving, Henry" (40).

Lloyd's announcement may be no more superfluous than his theatrical gesture of shooting Mae. The loop was already closed; as far as Mae was concerned,
they had already spiritually killed her. The insipid and incipient violence—
already evident in act 1, scene 1—would require a dramatically and theatrically
different context *not* to be realized. Mae's final speech resounds triumphantly
but reveals something closer to the truth. "Like a starfish," Mae says, "I live in
the dark and my eyes see only a faint light. It is faint and yet it consumes me. I
long for it. I thirst for it. I would die for it. Lloyd, I am dying" (40). Mae's self-
perception has been realized, according to her. She has become the spiritually
graced single entity she hungered to be. But she has achieved a solitariness that
echoes what was never communicative about her, what never reached honestly
for connection; she has been "consumed." Mae's coming into language, into
the power of art, at her death is so brief and the subtext so resonant that I see no
redemption of the self in this tragedy of human intercourse. Mae's death
confirms for both Mae and her audience the destructiveness of her life. While
Lloyd's ultimate violence confirms the violence she knows the men have done
to her all along, emotionally and intellectually, it also confirms her own self-
afflicted violence. Again, Mae's death only appears to be an explosion; rather, it
is her own implosion.

It is the play's general context rather than Mae's constructed text that is
finally at fault here. Her text was continually controlled by the theater, by the
conditions of always having to play against other characters and against the set.[7]
When, in 1986, Fornes revisioned Anton Chekhov's short story "Drowning" as
a one-act play of the same name, she essentially inverted the genre of the short
story, turned it inside out to expose the genre of drama; what is *visible* takes
precedence, finally, over any other element against which character is determined. In the critical context of poverty, of the impoverished man's alienation
from society, lonely and loveless, Fornes's play constructs an emotional center
through a visual image. The play uses the bare emotion of Chekhov's character—that is, a man so desperate for money and attention that he will drown
himself for a fee—and transforms the character into something other than what
is recognizably human, all feeling and all flesh:

> Heads . . . large and shapeless, like potatoes. . . . Their flesh is shiny and oily.
> Their eyes are reddish and watery. . . . When they breathe their bodies sweat.
> . . . Their skin and general shape resemble those of seals or sea lions. (57)

Fornes's set ("There is a lot of olive green in the air and the trimmings are olive
green enamel" [57]) evokes the place that Chekhov's character eventually goes,
a place where Chekhov's reader cannot go but where the drama's spectator *can*

go—underwater, where the character's emotion reaches its own apex. The play never explicitly acknowledges the plot of Chekhov's story but, rather, *images* the character's desperation that in Chekhov's story culminates in the ironic moment of "the end of the performance. Having 'drowned,' the individual climbs out of the water and, on receiving his thirty kopecks, walks off, wet and shivering with cold" (54). In Fornes's play the character drowns from the inside out, drowns from the excess of need, anguish, and emotion. As another character concludes, from the café table where the entire drama has taken place: "He's drowning. He hurts too much" (62). The stage space becomes, explicitly, the character's emotion realized in space. Fornes brings her spectators into that space in order to engage them as thoroughly as possible in the sequence of emotions that culminate in the play's final words. She represents, finally, how character can ultimately be defined by the space that character inhabits.

In *Mud* Mae is transformed into something virtually other than human in order to reveal the extent to which her own self-definition is dependent on context. "Mud" is Mae's emotion, her entire narrative, realized in stage space. The theater, for Fornes, is a place in which the artist can literalize context, foregrounding the visible world's impact on the individual and the visible world as the contrived product of individuals. The theatrical frame in *Mud* is so self-conscious, so crafted, that the spectator will be unable to forget the theater even while occupied with the narrative. The formal attributes of theater—the set, the scene breaks, the props—are exhibited in order to reveal that aspect of the human life that is theatrical. The institutional contexts that we construct, as we construct sets in the theater, will determine us as much as we determine them. The relationships between Mae, Lloyd, and Henry are subject to their world of poverty and ignorance, and herein lies *Mud*'s most political assertion. If we do not use language to deconstruct our institutions, then we will be bound to them. If we were to use language in honest response to our institutions, toward dismantling them, toward opposing them when they are oppressive, we could transform our worlds. But, as long as we play roles within the institutions we inhabit—as lovers, friends, students, teachers—without understanding our power to remake those institutions, without understanding our power as artists, there is no escaping their oppressive violence. Character is finally role-playing and stage-pacing. If Mae cannot destroy her own mud, her character will always be fixed. And, as character is defined against any other character on the stage, there is no self without the other; Lloyd and Henry, too desperate and ignorant to perceive themselves as capable of change, react with fear to this realization at the play's end and are, hence, ironically stirred to murder Mae in an effort to save themselves.

   While *Mud* reminds us of the devastating effects of violence that we cannot necessarily see, that is, violence to the human spirit, it is also a call to arms
to prevent the materialization of that violence. As the characters between scenes
explicitly share responsibility for the set, the spectator too is assigned responsibility for this theatrical text. If the spectator becomes seduced by plot, letting
narrative assert itself, then one's participation parallels Mae's, and the text will
continue to write itself. The spectator, like Mae and like the Chekhovian character in "Drowning," is also threatened with being consumed by his or her
environment. In Mae's case it is the larger theatrical text of poverty and ignorance that demands intercession. More and more explicitly in her ensuing dramas, Fornes demands that the spectator recognize the need to interrupt the
image-in-process.

4

Sarita

Sarita (1984) centers on the play's young eponymous heroine who, like so many of Fornes's female characters, plays the simultaneous roles of victim and victimizer, is both naive and wise, powerless and ultimately powerful. Fornes provides Sarita with a world significantly more expansive than Mae's mud and with more tools with which to work, though resemblances between the two spheres predominate: *Sarita*'s set—with the exception of a brief foray to the Empire State Building and a final scene in a mental hospital—is also conspicuously enclosed, though it is boxes rather than mud that contextualize this drama. The boxes allow more light and space into Sarita's world, are enlivened with music, cultural memorabilia, and bright colors, even while they, too, evoke their own limitations.

In the course of the drama Sarita gains both a husband and a child, Mark and Melo, though her affair with Julio, her lover since childhood and a man who has persistently manipulated and controlled her, has disabled any happiness in those relationships. Rather than finding power in her own capabilities or in relation to Mark or Melo, she uses power in the play's penultimate scene to murder Julio. And yet, although Sarita's story also ends tragically, her drama's progress has a vitality foreign to Mae's world. Perhaps coincident with Fornes's own developing art and reverence for its power, Sarita manages at moments to make art religious, to recognize its possibilities for conversion and redemption.

Sarita is a lonely and destructive woman snared both in the 1940s South Bronx and within the cultural expectations of her Hispanic community. This especially lyrical play—full of poetry in language, music, spectacle, and emotion—dramatizes her efforts to use ritual to disrupt that stubborn context. Sarita's complex mix of reverence and irreverence, care and carelessness, toward the rituals she engages in provides for the bulk of the play's dramatic and theatrical movement. In *From Ritual to Theatre: The Human Seriousness of Play* (1982) Victor Turner describes ritual:

essentially as *performance, enactment,* not primarily as rules or rubrics. The rules "frame" the ritual process, but the ritual process transcends its frame. . . . The term "performance" is . . . derived from Old English *parfournir,* literally "to furnish completely or thoroughly." To perform is thus to bring something about, to consummate something, or to "carry out" a play, order, or project. But in the "carrying out," I hold, something new may be generated. The performance transforms itself. (79)

Ritual is activity, "liminal," the performance of transition. Turner's "liminal phenomena" can coincide

with crises in social processes whether these result from internal adjustments or external adaptations or remedial measures. Thus they appear at . . . natural disjunctions in the flow of natural and social processes. They are thus enforced by sociocultural "necessity," but they contain *in nuce* "freedom" and the potentiality for the formation of new ideas, symbols, models, beliefs. (54)

At moments of crisis Sarita practices a kind of personalized process of liminal activity (unlike the more collective, communal activity for which Turner intends the term [80]), in efforts to explode the systems by which she feels determined. She does, indeed, seek to create new models and to disrupt her own and others beliefs, even if she is not fully cognizant of her own activity.

Turner elaborates on the process of ritual:

The rules may "frame" the performance, but the "flow" of action and inter-action within that frame may conduct to hitherto unprecedented insights and even generate new symbols and meanings, which may be incorporated into subsequent performances. (79)

While those around her participate in culturally dictated ceremonies, or "insti-tutionalized performance[s] of indicative, normatively structured social reality," Sarita attempts to transcend ceremony, which is "both a model *of* and a model *for* social states and statuses" (83), in order to inhabit ritual, the conduit for trans-formation of these implied models. At the play's end there is the possibility, at least, that Sarita has generated change.

Overall, however, she is both a success and failure at this enterprise, a truth underscored by Fornes's deliberate depiction of Sarita as insufficiently critical of her own ritualistic behavior, even while she condemns the ceremonies that sur-round her. The failure of certain personal rituals for Sarita is partly due to her failure to recognize, and subsequently to act against, the larger and more strict ceremonies of the society by which she is bound. She attempts to use spectacle, the stuff of ritual, to compel change, but too often she does so without dissecting the significance and impact of that spectacle and without either cognizance or the ability to affect herself as spectacle or the spectacle she makes of herself. Her rituals are insufficiently transformative because of her obstinate character. On the one hand, she is classically rebellious, unwilling to play either the role of mother, daughter, or lover according to any predictable script. On the other hand, she never dramatically attempts to transform her various contexts in order to affect those roles. While she snubs certain traditions, she is dangerously obedient to others. Though willing to abandon her child, for example, she does so only for the sake of returning to an abusive lover. Though her sustained defiance draws her closer in character to Fefu, her stubborn naïveté, spirituality, and selfishness align Sarita more with Mae and similarly condemn her to a life of lost chances.

The play, on one level, offers a classic love triangle, circumscribed by issues of race and by Sarita's search for liberation from the potentially confining roles of mother and wife. While the heroine devotes her sensuality (the best part of herself) to Julio, a man who will never love her properly, her Caucasian lover, Mark, devotes his altruism (the best part of himself) to Sarita. Nobody's needs will be satisfied, even as both Sarita and Mark struggle to give their best. Similarly, *Sarita* as a play is bound simultaneously to satisfy certain of the spectator's needs (the characters put on a great show) and to frustrate others (there is no possibility of a happy ending). *Sarita* teases its spectators with dramatic shifts in spectacle—of light, color, music, and dance— sometimes potent, sometimes impotent, that can be profoundly and irreverently mood altering. The subtext is almost always grave—the pain of unfulfilled desire, of immoral behavior, of loss—but the context is religious celebration, romance, sexual play, and theatrical games.

The seduction of the spectator can be gratifying; colorful and bold imagery, playful connections between characters, the voyeuristic pleasures of watching certain flirtations succeed, amount to the spectator's pleasure. But the seduction can be frustrating too; Fornes arrests her characters' sexual activity just before climax, their romances just before real love. Progress is often elusive. Though the eponymous heroine enacts a movement from innocence to guilt, Sarita remains a child by never fully entering into the adult world of productivity or responsibility, even while she enters certain of that world's trials and pains. Even Sarita's ultimate violence of the penultimate scene comes across as oddly anticlimactic. And the seduction, the withholding, is perfectly perpetuated by the play's final image, which, while it offers little in the way of closure, may (and only may) have affirmative social resonance beyond the otherwise cynical conclusion to the play.

Thematically, *Sarita* describes the tragedy of a "spirited young woman," age range thirteen to twenty-one, in the South Bronx of the 1940s, who is determined not to repeat her mother's mistakes and bound to repeat them if she cannot find her way out of her mother's social and political world, a world circumscribed by the poverty and inexperience of the offspring of immigrants.[1] Sarita's conflict, like her mother's (as we learn later in the play), is finally that she is unable to explore intellectual and creative aspects of herself, given her poverty and social restrictions, and hence her sense of self is determined by her relationships with men, particularly with her abusive lover, Julio, and his apparent inverse, the kindly Mark. Though Sarita takes pains not to blame her mother, the spectator can easily surmise the extent to which Sarita's self-definition is the consequence of the political world in which she lives, a world that her mother has been either unable or unwilling to elude, hence a world that repeats itself in Sarita's generation.

But Sarita is not her mother; rather, she is a typical Fornesian protagonist (like Fefu or Mae), a woman of significant spiritual depth with a poetic sensibility and an inclination toward articulating and pursuing her desires. Despite Sarita's youthfulness and a political situation as constraining as those of Fornes's other heroines, Sarita seems to have a certain measure of control over this drama. Because of the strength of her sensuality, she is more of an artist than Fornes's other heroines, more actively creative, more engaged in her environment. But her control, like Fefu's or even Mae's before her, is ominous; she has enough power to be as destructive as constructive. And, because Sarita is never properly trained or educated, her powers remain confined to a context she cannot alter, and she destroys each time she creates.

Sarita's relationship to every other character in the drama is that of a child to an adult (given that the spectator never sees Sarita with her child, her motherhood offers no threat to this characterization). She projects the voice of morality onto her mother, assigns responsibility for her actions to Julio and the responsibility for her redemption to Mark. By refusing the burden herself, Sarita compels her mother and Fernando (the family's boarder) to be responsible for her child, Melo, thereby eluding entirely the role of mother, at least as far as the spectator is concerned. Sarita blames the intensity of her desire for Julio for all of her actions, including abandoning Melo, being unfaithful to Mark, and eventually murdering Julio himself.

Fornes represents *Sarita*'s characters as especially naive. All of the characters in this drama simultaneously act both childish and adult. On the one hand,

Fornes embraces their childishness with affection (many characters in Fornes's plays are redeemed by their youthful perspectives); she celebrates their youthful tendencies toward spirituality and their lack of pretension. But, on the other hand, Fornes attributes characters' downfall to their callowness. While Emma from *Fefu,* for example, may typify Fornes's view of maturity (she owns her actions, exposes herself, and acts responsibly by considering her impact on others), Sarita never learns to step away from her needs in order to view herself more honestly. She appeals to others constantly—to God, to her mother, to Julio, to Mark—for guidance. At age nineteen in scene 14, out of twenty scenes, Sarita is still asking God for a sign. She is still unable to evaluate her own actions morally: "If one has one true love in one's lifetime," she asks, "only one, and one has been true to that love, does one go straight to heaven?" She even pretends to speak for God, lowering her voice to coddle herself: "Good lord, child, somebody made a mistake. . . . You're my favorite kid. Don't worry about a thing, honey" (126).

But Fornes, perhaps unlike her more skeptical and overly intellectual spectators, will not entirely condemn Sarita for her transgressions. As in *Mud,* context is as much at fault as are those who inhabit the context. And in this play respect for some aspects of context are rewarded; certain traditions demand deference from both Fornes and her characters. In *Sarita* Fornes offers a child's world wherein ritual is often enacted for its own sake, or for art's sake, as much as for whatever religious or spiritual goals it seeks to address. Hence, while irresponsible engagement in ritual will be destructive, faith in ritual is inherently redemptive in Sarita's world, as her mother, Fela, asserts in act 2's first scene, which opens amid a flurry of ritualistic celebration, with Fernando playing the skeptic:

> *Fernando:* . . . I want to make it clear that I don't believe in all this espiritismo and santeria. I'm a Catholic and I don't see why you have to give food to the Virgin.
> *Fela:* That's Oshun [the Virgin of La Caridad del Cobre (111)], Fernando.
> *Fernando:* That's a statue of the Virgin Mary.
> *Fela:* Yes, but it's Oshun. Give me the fritters.
>
> (112)

Even without the cooperation of her surrounding world, with the presence of skeptics and the wrong materials, Fela insists on practicing her ritual for ritual's sake. She insists on her own power to make what she sees into what she wants. Fornes celebrates the childish imagination that need not be powerless. As the theater more generally proves, art can be as powerful as it aims to be; it can convert the experience of the living into theater.

Respect for art makes Sarita significantly more empowered from the start than a character like Mae; context enables her to explore and fully engage in a wide range of rituals—linguistic, spiritual, musical, theatrical, sexual—as a way of seeking an elusive power over her own desire and her lover's misuse. Certainly, to some degree Sarita's forays into ritual continually fail her; each proves to be ultimately unproductive, given her goals. Sarita is finally led to try to seize control over her drama in a conclusive act of violence that is as much self-denying and generally destructive as it may be effective in scouring the stage of its worst evil. But Fornes, as always, has final say here; she does not allow the play's politics, momentous as they are, to dominate her theater. In *Sarita,* theatrically at the very least, ritual is a resounding success. It can transform scenes with the most painful of thematic subtexts into apparent celebrations of life or transform scenes of devastating hopelessness into humor. And, ultimately, the overarching ritual of this play—the creation of drama, of active artistic reshaping—may transform the distressing ending to one that instead suggests a play beyond this play, in which the power of ritual knows no bounds. Though one extended family is seemingly destroyed—the unit of Sarita's mother, child, two lovers, and self—another potential family seems to be in only its most incipient stages. The playwright's ritual, the artist's privilege, enables Fornes to restage her characters on the threshold of change. She suggests that her play and her playwriting are not ceremonies but rituals.

The play begins and ends in two very different physical spaces. Where the play concludes, a sitting room in a mental hospital, illustrates Sarita's fall from innocence. Yet Sarita is still a child at the play's end, accepting chocolate from Fernando (132). And, though the space of Fela's colorful living room could not differ more from the somber mental hospital, Fornes uses the latter space much as Sarita uses the former. Fornes closes the drama by hinting at a new familial union between Sarita, Fernando, and Mark, evoking the reworking of family dynamics that children do with dolls. Though drastically refigured, this theatrical event is still transpiring in the dollhouse evoked in the play's first act.

Sarita's set is a series of boxes piled like toys, one smaller and recessed (Sarita's tenement kitchen where she lives after she leaves her mother and child), above the larger one, which is Fela's living room.[2] The brightness of the set, the brilliant lighting, colorful furniture and clothing, the high walls and overstuffed chairs, suggest a diorama or a dollhouse. Music emanates from behind the set like a music box, and the small windows at the top of the high walls could seem to be handles. The first scene opens on two girls, Sarita and her friend Yeye, playing in their parochial school uniforms, perpetuating the sense of a dollhouse. The play begins in a child's world, wherein two children attempt to manipulate their fate through fortune-telling, raising the question of who really controls their fate, that is, who is playing with these particular dolls. The first scene, titled "Fortune Telling" (93), is appropriately prophetic; this is a world in which a child's imagination and spirituality struggle with larger forces for satisfaction of desire.

Yeye's fortune-telling and Sarita's participation evoke a system both arbitrary and orderly, a pattern but a mysterious and mystical pattern. Sarita and Yeye's discourse is immediately both penetrable and impenetrable. The spectator is accosted with a fluid and poetic series of words, "merengue . . . big love . . . rice pudding . . . butterfly," which are the words that accompany Yeye's reading of Sarita's cards. Yeye speaks quickly and confidently, making a kind of consistent sense as she moves methodically through all fifty-two cards, correcting the cards' errors ("teenth which is teeth"), but both the aural spectator and Sarita are still kept somewhat at bay: "31-Rita. Who is Rita?" Yeye asks (93). Neither Sarita nor the spectator knows. As their ritual continues, however, the spectator becomes aware of the ritual as Yeye and Sarita's efforts to control their drama, making the discourse comprehensible at least in a general way. Though at moments their work appears to be purely and simply child's play, at others the gravity of the story the cards tell is unmistakable. While Yeye's playfulness can be what is most distracting—"One, two, three. Quarter, quarter, quarter. He loves you," she concludes while tapping the cards (94)—the scene ends on a significantly ominous note, when Yeye drops a card as she leaves:

> (. . . *She starts to pick it up and stops. She looks at it.*)
> *Sarita:* What is it?
> *Yeye: (Picking it up.)* Nothing.
>
> (97)

The scene's thematic subtext portends danger. Both Sarita and the spectator know from the outset that reality conflicts with her desires; Julio is unfaithful, and Sarita's desire is desperate. Sarita has apparently seen Julio with another girl, and, though she asks Yeye and the cards, "What was he doing with her?" (94), she is the one who provides the answer: "his thing [was] standing up" (95)—he was flirting sexually with the other girl. Sarita's response to her knowledge is terrible and poignant: "I think I'm dying," she tells Yeye. "—He takes my life with him when he leaves me" (97).

What Sarita wants from this ritual is not insight into her affairs, either into Julio's motives or what constitutes her continued desire for him. She is a child, and what she wants, therefore, is simply the power to alter the course of events. Sarita does not want her fortune told; she wants her fortune changed by the ritual of the telling. But unwilling, or unable, to do more than speak mystically to the cards, to close her eyes and wish for Julio's fidelity and to spend her money on Yeye's telling Sarita only what she wants to hear, Sarita remains doomed to her fate.

The ritual will necessarily be unproductive in the manner Sarita desires; Yeye cannot cast a spell on Julio, nor can Sarita's wishing alone help her to achieve her goals. The spectacle of the "Fortune Telling" scene, however, tells a very different story than does the text. The predominant theatrical image is of the playfulness and gaiety of these staged rituals. The entire scene is nearly overwhelmed not only with the spectacle of fortune-telling but with music and dance as well. Yeye's song, "He Was Thinking of You" (95–96), and Sarita's song, "I'm Pudding" (96), carry the potential gravity of their concerns merrily along. Though Yeye constructs for Sarita a most unlikely set of explanations for Julio's behavior ("He called you. / You weren't home. . . . / She came along. / He was thinking of you, . . . / He didn't notice / He got aroused"), and Sarita's song belies her childish romanticism ("I'm at school. . . . / I think of him and I'm pudding"), both do so in the context of children at play, singing and dancing almost joyfully. Together the two girls sing "Holy Spirit, Good Morning" (96–97), which leaves their particular concerns far behind for the sake of the spiritual indulgence that their music provides. The celebratory rituals of song and dance render the text subtext to the extensive theatricality. Though the text culminates in Sarita's declaration: "I think I'm dying. . . . I'm going to do what he does. I'm going out with every guy I meet" (97), belying the uselessness of their ritual at least on the level of Sarita's drama, ritual has been productive on the level of *Sarita*'s theatrical stage.

While Sarita's disturbing political reality continues to be delineated in the next few scenes, spectacle remains carelessly oblivious to its relationship to that text. Yeye's vague prophecy at the end of the last scene has come true for the moment, at least in the content of the first incongruous image of act 1, scene 2. Sarita lies on the sofa in a child's posture, head hanging over the edge toward the floor, feet up on the sofa's back, still in her school uniform; her words, however, immediately reveal the extent to which that youthful image is deceptive: "I'm pregnant" (98), Sarita tells her mother. Fela and Sarita process the stages of denial, anger, despair, and, finally, understanding and acceptance. And Sarita offers a succinct summary of events:

> Mami, I was crying all the time. I was unhappy. . . . Julio left me. . . . You can't think of anything when you're unhappy like that. I went with boys and I felt better. (99)

Her story is familiar enough: Julio's rejection of Sarita resulted in a profound insecurity and self-loathing, "cured" by proving herself attractive to other men. She insists her mother is not at fault, but she does not blame Julio. Instead, she blames herself: "You taught me right. . . . I'm a savage" (100). Fela's solution is the conventional marriage ceremony; she tries to arrange for Sarita to become Fernando's wife. Though the issue is undeniably grave—that is, what to do with a fourteen-year-old unwed mother—the mood evoked by the song Sarita, Fela, and Fernando sing in concert is irreverent at best. Though Fernando is an old man, his lyrics are a child's:

> I need someone who'll tuck me in.
> Someone who'll guard my sleep.
> Someone who'll ask me how I feel.
>
> (103)

Sarita and Fela provide Fernando with a chorus, answering his "I'm saying that I'm lonely./ . . . Don't tell me that I am not" with "He's saying that he's lonely./ . . . Don't tell him that he's not" (101). This is pure theater, the performers keenly aware of their audience. Verse and chorus are repetitive and playful and the lyrics nearly inane. But what the characters are having fun with is difficult to unravel. The song mocks the transpiring events *and* mocks itself, drawing attention to itself as form and effectively trivializing its own content. The ambiguous directions to the audience about what to take seriously and what to disregard are part of the spectators' seduction. They are kept, as it were, on the edge of their seats, not yet qualified to comprehend the correlations between form and content, waiting for a sign.

The spectator walks a fine line in terms of analysis: again, the subtext is grave; the context is frivolous. Fela's song, "A Woman like Me" (103–4), is at the very least melodramatic, if not trite. She sings:

> A woman like me
> loves a man, only one,

and he must
run away.
He must forsake her.
He must forget her.
He must betray her.

(104)

There is no playful spectacle to contextualize Fela's song; rather, she sits on the couch throughout the entire song, a scene unto itself, singing her ballad solemnly to the audience. Insofar as Fela's song only makes more specific the complexities of Sarita's conflict, it offers very little to the drama's—let alone the theatrical event's—progress.

The passivity that characterizes Fela through the lyrics of "A Woman like Me" will contrast significantly with Sarita's character. By the end of the scene in which Fela is trying to arrange a marriage for Sarita, Sarita has seized dramatic and theatrical control amid the mounting musical frenzy by interrupting with: "I'll support him [her child]. You take care of him. *And you too. And I'll support him*" (103), to Fela and Fernando. Though the audience is in a position to wonder at the practicality of Sarita's solution (it resembles too much her earlier solution of promiscuity to "cure" her loneliness; neither shows self-analysis or any awareness of the impact she is having on the lives of others), Sarita's activity reverberates theatrically in comparison to Fela's passivity. Following Fela's overdramatic and self-pitying song, sung from where she is firmly planted on the couch, comes Sarita's departure from the world of Fela's living room. Sarita implicitly offers her abandonment of her mother and child (two years have passed) as an alternative to her mother's passivity. Though it is not much of an alternative—her activity notwithstanding, she is abandoning her child and only in order to return to Julio—given the context, there is something triumphant in Sarita's movements. She is dressed in her coat and beret, while her mother sleeps pathetically on the couch in her housecoat. When she whispers to her sleeping mother: "I'll send [Melo] money. Don't worry, Mami. I'll take care of myself" (105), the spectator is not in a position righteously to insist that Sarita stay in the world dramatized here.

The next scene, act 1, scene 6, acts as a bridge into a kind of ritualization of sexuality. Sexuality, for Fornes, is often its own text and its own spectacle; it shows and tells its own story. Sex is ritualistic for Sarita, and for *Sarita,* in that it transforms the narrative; while Sarita's drama continues on its way to an ultimate degeneration, the sexual energy of Sarita's unions with Julio pervades the play's semiotics. Sexuality's powers of ritual are not without irony or destructive qualities, however; the transformations achieved are ambiguous.

Lacking the spectacular qualities of music and dance, the play stalls for the next four scenes, confined to the unwavering space of Sarita's kitchen. As if to replace music and dance, sexual activity is the foundation of these scenes' tableaux. After the bridge scene the literary narrative, too, has a stubborn prevalence, even while there is little dramatic development and notable repetition.

The first of these four scenes is essentially a photograph still—textless and therefore compelling the spectator to heed spectacle entirely. Act 1, scene 6, offers no more than an image of Sarita and Julio carefully posed. Engaged as the spectators have been in the veritable chaos of aural, musical spectacle, they are now forced to arrest those pleasures abruptly, to heed what they see rather than what they hear. As spectacle had provided a lens for the narrative, distorting or clarifying, in earlier scenes, now the image itself is the entire text. The characters at this dramatic moment are as close as they can be to two-dimensional, which may make the spectator more willing to embrace them as three-dimensional—that is, as "real"—at later moments in the drama. Or this ruse may be a reminder that none of this is, in fact, real. This is art, and the frame must be considered. This is how someone, playwright or character, *wants* the image to look.

Fornes also suggests that this is how the spectator wants the image to look, that the image satisfies the spectator's expectations. Sarita and Julio are looking into a mirror, and the audience, then, is cast as their reflection. Or they are cast as the audience's reflection; Sarita and Julio could even be dressed for the theater, Sarita in her dress and beret, Julio in his double-breasted suit. The metatheatrical implication is that the spectator is as responsible for this image as any other participant in this theatrical event.

The causal ambiguities of that relationship between character and spectator are enhanced by the certainty that a mirror image can never reflect the precise truth. As Shakespeare's Richard II learns, every reflected image is necessarily a distortion of the primary image. That this image is strikingly clean and attractive suggests an idealization of Sarita and Julio's relationship, consistent enough with Sarita's desires. But this is also the playwright's view. Both perspectives demand that any analysis of Sarita's actions be subject to an evaluation of that brief, framed image. As part of the playwright's ritual, the making of images in process in order to affect the spectator's perceptions, this moment speaks to the power of ritual precisely in transforming perception. The next three scenes—each essentially a variation of this still, accompanied by brief text and by fervent sexual exchanges between Sarita and Julio—give the spectators time to adjust their vision, even to concentrate on the act of observation.

"The Mirror" scene brings the characters and spectators into Sarita's kitchen, the second space above the "primary" space of Fela's living room. Not unlike the telescoping space in Fornes's *The Conduct of Life,* these different the-

atrical spaces both echo each other and explore similar themes in different physical realms. Sarita's kitchen is not her mother's house—that fact is essential in
further distinguishing Sarita's drama from Fela's—but her activities therein,
with Julio and later Mark, comment on what one might imagine was her
mother's younger life. The extent to which both women are/were dependent
on men is explored, compared and contrasted, in both spaces.

Sarita distinguishes herself from her mother with sexual activity and by trying to articulate her feelings in relation to Julio. The next three scenes each
begin with Sarita writing a letter to Julio and reading the letter aloud to the
audience. By the third scene (act 1, sc. 9), the act is a ceremony for both Sarita
and her spectators. Thematically, Sarita's letters describe her efforts to distance
herself from Julio; she tries to delineate in each what his abuse has done to her,
and she becomes increasingly successful at the task. The first is characterized by
anger and denial; the second more explicitly blames Julio, more elaborately
articulates her own pain, but also perpetuates the extent to which Sarita has
internalized her pain by converting it into self-loathing and cynicism; the third
letter, two scenes but a full year later, indicates that Sarita has become more
cognizant of her condition, even while she stubbornly clings to the self-loathing
it inspires. Sarita is attempting to use language—rather than any other element
of spectacle, rather than any of the more arresting arts of earlier scenes—to free
herself from the particular bondage of her relationship with Julio. But the lack
of progress from letter to letter, over a year and a half, reveals the tenacity of
Sarita's bondage. Thematically, the spectator encounters a child writing desperate letters to an audience whose inattention is ensured (Julio never reads them),
ultimately as passive and unproductive as her mother had been.

That narration stagnation is once again countered by a theatrical diver-
gence. Sarita's letter-writing ceremony is accompanied in two of these three
scenes by the ritual of her lovemaking with Julio. As Sarita and Yeye's song and
dance in the first scene forced the subtext to resonate differently, so does the
spectacle of sex for these scenes. On the one hand, the eroticism of these scenes
contrasts the loneliness of Sarita's texts. But that eroticism also provides context
and, as such, can force Sarita's words to resonate fervently; the scenes become
less about Sarita's seclusion than about her relationship, even her alliance, with
Julio.

Though Sarita's text belies her lack of control, the images the spectators
encounter here are very controlled, as if to underscore Fornes's artistic ritual.
The simple set is powerful in and of itself (as in the INTAR [International Arts
Relations] performance cited in the endnotes). Sarita wears a red dress, Julio a
yellow shirt, both of which set off the green chairs. Within this vivid space

Sarita and Julio's physical movements are neatly choreographed. An orderliness to the image is reinforced by the scene's predictability. In each scene Sarita waits for Julio to return, surreptitiously unlocks the door to enable his entrance, is teased by Julio, who will not read her letters, and is eventually sexually seduced by him. The spectator can assume a certain repetition.

The spectator cannot assume that either of these scenes will reach any climax or epiphany. A lack of sexual closure, as it were, parallels a lack of emotional or intellectual progress for Sarita and Julio:

> *The lights fade to black. Sarita emits orgasmic sounds. There are the sounds of struggle and fall. . . . The stage is lit. Sarita stands on the up left corner. Julio kneels on the floor. He holds on to her.* (106–7)

Sarita withholds Julio's orgasm and, indirectly, the spectator's satisfaction.

The spectator's experience of the playwright's control of these scenes should resemble Sarita's experience of Julio's control. What may originally seem erotic comes to seem pornographic through this careful control of the image and subsequent teasing of both the spectator and the characters. These exchanges between Sarita and Julio are still lifes, often explicitly framed for the spectator by the set. In act 1, scene 8, for example, Sarita and Julio's lovemaking occurs within the frame of the legs of the table. The sporadic brightening and fading of the lights controls the spectator's gaze, often specifically in order to prevent the spectator from seeing the fruition of Sarita and Julio's sexual activities. Similarly, each time we watch Sarita write a note, we come to understand it as foreplay to a sexual encounter with Julio, seducing the audience further just as Sarita and Julio are seduced by each other.[3]

Fornes casts her spectators as Sarita's voyeurs, particularly as the theatrical space is foregrounded as Sarita's space—so the audience, like Julio, distinctly enters *her* space for gratification of some kind. It is a violation of Sarita, a wresting of her control over these dramatic events. She has tried to make her letter writing and her sexual encounters with Julio transformative rituals, but the more powerful forces of playwright, director, audience, and Julio (who is himself a little of all three) deform Sarita's success. Her only hope of breaking the pattern will be to forgo these particular rituals. Unfortunately, however, that act is a passive one for Sarita. She neither analyzes nor carefully rejects her patterns but simply steps away from them.

After she writes her third letter Sarita leaves before Julio arrives, denying the spectators the ritual they have come to anticipate. Hence, just before the scene that will end act 1, even the tentative satisfaction of the two previous scenes is not proffered, which both perpetuates and shifts the seduction. In the last scene, in which Sarita is saved from her suicide by Mark's romantic love, the drama undergoes the significant change of reemphasized visual spectacle, a change in scene to the backdrop of the Empire State Building, a reprieve from the repetition of the preceding scenes—an overall reinvigoration.

That reanimation notwithstanding, what the scene offers is not entirely a dramatic step forward, even if it is a theatrical step forward. Clichés and conventions abound. The scene is standardly romantic. Mark not only saves Sarita from suicide by acting the perfect stranger but also, stage directions indicate, falls in love (109). He sings a quintessential romantic song to Sarita, "You Are Tahiti," which insists:

> You are the flower.
> I am the snow.
> You are Tahiti.
> I am Gauguin.
>
> (109)

Certain traditions of film and theater are so intact they invite suspicion. The Empire State Building as a site for a suicide attempt is a cliché; Mark has fallen in love with the essence of the victimized and needy woman, and Sarita has found her shining knight. Or she has cast her shining knight. "You are so nice.—I know you're nice" (109), she says, revealing that Mark is what she wants him to be above all else; he is the answer to her need projected, effectively deus ex machina. Both insist they are saved from selflessness. Mark sings: "I, without you, / am but a void," and Sarita responds to his song with, "Do you know that . . . without you I would have died?" (110). These romantic clichés immediately make suspect the validity of Sarita and Mark's relationship, ending the first act on a skeptical note. But the mood is happy, Sarita and her spectators have eluded Julio's presence however temporarily, we are in a new place, and the scene reflects genuine hopefulness.

With the beginning of act 2 we reenter the world of spectacular ritual. Back in Fela's living room, the set is festive: *"[Sarita] and Fela decorate an altar to Oshun (the Virgin of La Caridad del Cobre). They wear party clothes. There are conga drums on the up left corner of the stage"* (111). The convivial mood set by the romantic discovery of Sarita and Mark at the end of act 1 carries smoothly into the first scene of act 2 (by far the longest and most complicated scene in the play), as Sarita tells her mother about Mark. There is little at the scene's onset to undermine the gaiety (except Sarita's continued infantilization, the implicit contrast of Mark with Julio, and the skepticism that may, given the conventions of the "Empire State Scene," surround ceremony at this point). The relationship Sarita has with Mark apparently could not be more different than her relationship with Julio—void of pain and possibly void of some kind of passion as well. "I met an American boy and I like him," Sarita tells Fela. "He thinks I am the greatest thing in the world. . . . We go where I want. . . . He brings me flowers. . . . He's a cutie pie" (111). Mark gives Sarita a sense of power and improved self-esteem. The first song for this scene is Sarita's playful and flirtatious "A Little Boo Boo," which demands, "Put a little kiss here / . . . . Take away this boo-boo / boo du du du" (111–12). The scene erupts into music and dance, in English and Spanish, in celebration of a religious holiday and, indirectly, of Sarita's newfound happiness. Fela and Fernando have their exchange about the statue of the Virgin Mary, which celebrates ritual and helps to undermine the overly intellectual spectator's doubts. Fela answers to the cynics that Sarita and Mark's romance is exactly as romantic as they want it to be.

While Sarita and Mark happily dance a foxtrot, they engage in banter that appears to have become a tradition for them. They tease each other cleverly and flirtatiously as if they were performing a scripted routine for an audience (indeed, Fernando, Juan, and Fela have stopped dancing and watch the lovers from the couch). Of young men from Cleveland (where Mark is from), Sarita asks with healthy cultural curiosity: "What do they say when they like a girl?" and Mark answers, "They say Oo! Loo-loo-loo-loo-loo!" And Sarita: "And is it true that they are all preachers' sons? . . . And is it true that they are all evangelists?" (114). But the pleasantries of their routine are quickly undone by Julio's entrance, their ceremony now framed once again by the larger cultural and gendered conventions to which they are bound. Sarita and Mark's exchange comes to seem no more than a trifling game in the face of Sarita's continuing conflict with Julio, in which she still plays a submissive part, despite her anger. Mark and Sarita stop dancing when they see Julio (and do not start up again):

> *Julio:* Go ahead, dance, dance. I don't care if you dance.
> *Sarita:* I don't care if you dance either. Go ahead, dance.—I was dancing before you came. I didn't ask if I could. Did I?
>
> (115)

The ominous and wishful subtext of Sarita's opening speech from this scene ("He likes me, you know. I know he likes me") cannot be ignored now. Sarita has been trying to use words, in speech and in music, to shape her relationship with Mark and to help her deny her relationship with Julio. But the ineffable

elements of the latter relationship—what the spectators see when they watch
the pair's ardent and painful lovemaking—suggest that Sarita's efforts to ritual-
ize her relationship with Mark, to transform it through music, through insistent
chanting of a kind, is to no avail.

Later in act 2 Sarita and Mark engage in similar literary banter as that of the
act's opening but with none of the high-spiritedness and little of the cleverness
of this first exchange. Rather, their discourse misses each other instead of forging any connection—and their differences are underscored as cultural: they do
not speak the same language. Discussing a woman who has passed out on the
beach of the summer resort they are visiting, Mark asks, "You can die from
doing a conga?" to which Sarita replies, "No, you can't die from doing a conga
but neither does empacho sound like tango." "Well, I don't think she went in
the water. She was fully dressed" (125), Mark concludes. This is not the verbal
lovemaking of earlier. Sarita and Mark's miscommunications testify to the distance that has developed between them since not only their conflicts but also
those of Sarita and Julio became Mark and Julio's. Though they stop short of
physical sparring, Mark and Julio predictably struggle for power over these
staged events. But what is unpredictable is that the struggle, characterized by
value judgments burdened with racial and social prejudices (Mark criticizes
Julio for not working; Julio calls Mark "nothing but a clean shirt!" [116]), leads
finally to more music and dance, though of a dramatically different tone than
what has preceded this change of scene.

The stage space is converted from the site of Fela's religion to Mark's religion. Mark sings "His Wonderful Eye" from above and behind the set (his
shadow is seen in the upper left window), while Sarita and Julio stand staring at
each other. The song is generically religious, in contrast to Fela's ethnically
specific religion. "For the lord / speaks in darkness," Mark sings. "And I see his
face / and his face says follow me" (116). Mark is not only spatially removed
from the drama but also spiritually removed; he does not belong in this world.
And yet, since his song provides a kind of voiced-over narration to Julio and
Sarita's reunion, he seems to exercise some control over this world. In fact,
locating him above and behind the set figuratively puts the puppet strings in
Mark's hands, makes him the child playing with this dollhouse. If the ceremonies of Sarita and Julio's socioeconomic and ethnic world are transcendent
insofar as the two end the scene together, singing a mournful lost-love song,
"Here Comes the Night," and their reunion is as inevitable as it was in the letter-writing scenes, still, as long as Mark's voice, or even the shadow of his presence, remains part of the spectacle, control lies neither in the hands of Sarita nor

Julio. As the traditions of Sarita and Julio's world keep Sarita subordinate to Julio, separate from Mark, and the power struggle confined to the men, the larger theatrical ritual keeps these characters bound to the drama rather than to their politics. Mark's removed presence evokes the omnipotent playwright who, by controlling spectacle, controls the characters' lives and the spectators' responses. The play insists that the course of events are out of everybody's hands, the characters' and spectators', as all are thrown back and forth by the apparent whimsy of spectacle or by the powers of what manipulates that spectacle.

For the time being the playwright seems to be seducing the spectator into valuing Sarita and Julio's relationship above Sarita and Mark's by appreciating, even idealizing, Sarita's passion, which ultimately targets Julio. When Fela and Yeye discuss their own lives as women in their world, they tell similar stories. Fela divulges her husband's abandonment of her when she was pregnant with Sarita, and Yeye responds that she knows her husband will leave her now that she is pregnant. She intimates that Sarita's story is the inverse of their own. Yeye tries to make some generalizations about men and women but ends up drawing attention to Sarita as the exception. She explains that, despite her imminent loss of a husband,

> I want to have a baby just the same. . . . Men are like that, Fe. . . . They don't feel like women that they want to have a baby. . . . Men don't have that need. . . . For them it's a weight on their backs. . . . For women too. . . . But they don't mind. They want the baby and it's part of them. Things are tough for women.—They are tough for men too because they don't understand it. . . . It's not their fault, that's how God made them. (119)

Sarita's quick and easy abandoning of her child for the sake of her love of the father (or possible father at least) removes Sarita from Yeye's idea of womanhood. Though the adult Sarita knows what she should want to want by Yeye's standards—as she tells God in her monologue, "God, I want to love Mark and no one else" (126)—she is still the child Yeye evokes when she tells Fela of Sarita's response to a nun from their childhood who talked about obedience. "She'd go on her knees and cry," Yeye says of Sarita, "and say, I want to be obedient, Yeye, I want to obey. . . . I want to obey I want to obey I want to obey I want to obey I want to obey" (119). As a child, Sarita had tried to make a religion out of her desire to be righteous, chanting her will to obey much as, for an example, she tries, as an adult, to compel her own moral behavior through her letters to Julio. But it is precisely the depth of Sarita's ardor and desires that distinguishes her; though her targets are dangerous, unlike Yeye and Fela's, Sarita's relationships are emotionally powerful, rather than the means to survival Yeye and Fela's marriages appear to be.

In this light her relationship with Mark comes too close to protocol. What is conventionally desirable about Sarita's relationship with Mark, and the rituals they engage in, cannot compete with what is otherwise desirable about Sarita's relationship with Julio—and the rituals *they* engage in. The controlled chaos of music, dance, text, and sex is finally a kind of minefield of spectacle in which the spectator must tread cautiously. That Sarita is able to express her sexuality through her relationship with Julio deserves approbation; it gives Sarita vitality when other women of her world are so consistently denied it. The cost, however, to echo the women of *Fefu and Her Friends,* may be Sarita's spirit.

The playwright actively reemerges at this point in the drama precisely in order to save Sarita's spirit. The theater may offer a context in which desire can be controlled; as Fornes has controlled the spectator's desire, she now intervenes to affect her characters' desires. Just before the play's violent climax and conclusion, Fornes offers a calm glimpse into the potential power of the theater. Sarita finds Fernando sitting in Fela's dark living room. Fernando's explanation of why he sits in the dark, and what he does there, evokes the theater:

> *Sarita:* Doesn't it bother you to sit in the dark? . . . What do you think of when you sit like this?
> *Fernando:* I imagine things. . . . I imagine that things are peaceful. That people go to work, and come back from work, and they eat and go to sleep.
>
> (128)

Fernando elaborates on the relevance of his imaginative exercises. For him cultural significance has been foremost. In the process he has become "an American." Though for years he had thought of and imagined "my island . . . the porch in my parents' house," one day he "thought of the people here. I imagined that you came home from school and you did your homework and that you didn't get into fights in the street." Fernando's imagination has at the very least provided him with respite from pain, even an inner peace, whether or not reality has realized his desires. But Sarita has no such access to the transformative power of her own imagination. Though she tells Fernando that she too "spend[s] time in a place that's far away," it is not a place that either she or the spectator can see:

> I wish I could think like you. I think of many things, but never quiet things. My heart is restless and I think of things that hurt me. They frighten me. I

feel pain in my chest. I am in danger. Teach me how to be like you. Teach
me how to look for peace. My heart won't let me. (128)

Sarita has no control over her own vision; she has no control over her artistic
self, which denies her the ability to construct any ritual that is truly her own,
personal and creative. She remains bound by Mark's ceremonies on one end of
the spectrum (romantic tradition, the possibility of convention and safety in
marriage and family) and Julio's on the other (expressed sexuality and emotion),
but with Sarita's inevitable subordination in a relationship determined by prejudices of their particular cultural, socioeconomic context.

Sarita never becomes the artist that the depth of her spirit suggests she
could be, though she still plays her role in a drama that clears the stage for a new
creative endeavor. Sarita is Fornes's tool—the victim who ends her victimization with a violent break from her bondage and, in so doing, reveres the power
of the playwright's art.

Sarita and Julio's relationship has inevitably devolved to the relationship
between a client and her prostitute. After their last sexual encounter Julio asks
Sarita for money:

You don't want me to tell Mark—you give me some money. . . . So you like
to hit the hay with me—so I have to eat. . . . Don't give me that lady stuff. I
know you ain't no lady. (129)

Sarita kills Julio by stabbing him when he tries to kiss her again, but the play
does not end with her violence. The penultimate "Death Scene" is followed by
a scene in which Fernando, and eventually Mark, visit Sarita at the mental hospital. Her murdering of Julio has not ended the drama but, instead, provided
space for both a dramatic and a theatrical shift. In the alliance of Sarita and Fernando the newly set stage becomes a place for a nontraditional relationship
between characters who are not tied by predictable or familiar conventions.
Though Fernando acts paternally toward Sarita, the play has offered no traditions for that relationship; its components remain to be determined. Further-
more, the spectator sees neither Sarita's mother nor her son, liberating Sarita
from the expectations of the roles of daughter and mother. The stage becomes
a place for different relationships between characters, a place in which label
alone does not determine role. Even the Sarita who sits before us is not the
woman we have known. She has achieved the unenviable distance from herself
that only madness can induce. She tells Fernando to keep Melo away from the
hospital:

> Don't let her near him. She's going to hurt him. Don't let her hurt him. She
> has done enough harm.—It's this thing I have inside me. Something I can-
> not tear off. It is a bad growth that will not die. (132)

And certainly, to some extent, Sarita has done enough harm—to herself, her
family, her son, even to Julio.

Though the play subsequently does not end with any personal triumph for
Sarita, it does project the possibility of a distinctly different future. Fornes completes the family Fernando and Sarita are constructing by bringing Mark back
onto the stage. "You came to see me? Even after what happened?" Sarita asks.
"I knew you were nice. I always knew it," she says and concludes, "What do
you think will happen?" an unanswered question that must compel the spectator to look beyond the end of this drama. While the penultimate scene achieved
its own closure, the ultimate scene essentially rewrites the play's ending, putting
the direction of the drama directly into the playwright's hands. Ritual for
Fornes is the *art* of religion; ritual can be truly transformative because the
"higher power" appealed to is an actual power within the seeker of change. The
artist who knows her goals, who practices ritual for the sake of both form and
context, has power enough to save the lives of her characters and to proffer the
possibility of that kind of power to the artists—to everyone—in her audience.

The Conduct of Life

The death of Orlando, an army lieutenant whose military success has coincided with his mastery of torturing political prisoners, may be punishment not only for the abuse that characterizes each of his human encounters throughout *The Conduct of Life* (1985) but also for his abuse of the theater. He commandeers the theatrical space he shares with the other characters, forces Nena, his stolen child-mistress, into one space and denies Leticia, his wife, access there. He is a brutal director, deliberately thwarting Leticia's smallest actions, ridiculing and humiliating her. His acting is pompous and arrogant, scene stealing, and he is killed just short of showstopping altogether. The political use Orlando makes of the theater comes down to force; both his audience and fellow players are captive.

As a Latin American military lieutenant and esteemed torturer, Orlando's respect for the power of the theater—of playing for an audience—is appropriate, if distorted. Fornes would like her spectators, in turn, also to respect the theater's semiotic powers. Hence, she constructs a theatricality for *Conduct* that wholly embraces the theater's multidimensioned frame. In this particularly sophisticated and powerful work, Fornes concerns herself most directly with theater as an artistic ritual that can in its own right offer passage out of the cycles of pain and abuse perpetuated by certain institutions. As Fornes intervened in Sarita's drama, the spectator is invited to consider the possibility of intervening in the violent world evoked by the dramatic world of this play.

In his essay, *"Still playing games:* Ideology and Performance in the Theater of Maria Irene Fornes" (1989) W. B. Worthen suggests that *Conduct,* as well as other of Fornes's plays:

> precisely address the process of theater, how the authority of the word, the presence of the performer, and the complicity of the silent spectator articu-

late dramatic play. . . . [L]ike dramatic action, theatrical action—performance—occupies an ideological field. (167–68)

The story of Orlando's various abuses and the responses from the women of the
household—Leticia, Nena, and Olimpia, the maid—are both told through the
theater and constructed by the theater; and, like the proverbial falling tree in the
unpeopled forest, the significance is in the hearing, in that meaning brought to
the event by the spectator's reception.

   Conduct is a series of tableaux organized around the human voice, the
human body, set design, lightness and darkness, and the general use of stage
space. Any and all textual meaning must be determined in the context of
Fornes's calculated use of these elements of spectacle. Both dramatic and political meaning are subject to the waves of spectacle on which the production of
the play relies, and, both dramatically and politically, the construction of character *and* spectator is explicitly determined by that spectacle. Fornes's use of
spectacle is not just a lens through which to scrutinize a literary text but a device
that transforms the drama into the production of a complex political concept. In
Fornes's play we look not only at but through spectacle, in part to understand
how it works, how looking is itself a political act. The ultimate effect of this
process has feminist implications; in *Conduct* women are the primary spectators
of the spectacles of themselves and their world. It is precisely within their roles
as spectators that they have power to affect spectacle, to produce political
change.

   The relationship of ultimate importance in this play is between the "actor"
and the "spectator," roles inhabited interchangeably by the characters, a process
that complicates the untangling of causality. Literary and theatrical readings support the view that play images the reverberating effects of violence. But
attempts to identify causal relationships between characters' actions, or between
events in the play, are subject to a theatrical reading that is problematic to a literary reading. The play never adheres consistently to a particular political ideology, but it does adhere to a theatrical ideology: the production insists that its
primary players—the actors/characters and the audience—are directly responsible for the play's politics. Finally, it is the political content of that relationship,
between character and spectator, that engenders the play's politics on literary,
dramatic, and theatrical levels alike.

   The first five scenes of *Conduct* plunge the spectator into a pattern of
significant contrasts, of nearly impenetrable darkness and spacious lightness,
sound and silence, stillness and furious, physical violence. The male and female
voice are contrasted, and through them anger and fear, power and subservience,

reason and emotion, are all (sometimes unexpectedly) represented. Silence and articulation are weighed against each other, as are the noises of the human voice without language and the noises of the human voice through language. The complexity of these contrasts is paralleled by the construction of a set that relies on the use of light and shadow for illumination of its meaning at any particular point and relies as well on what the human body does within that space, ranging from the miming of activity to intense emotional violence to enacted physical violence. In turn the spectator is likely to experience anything from laughter to pity to anger to terror. And all this in the space of the first five scenes—say, twenty minutes into production.

This powerful fluctuation of dramatic and theatrical mood can defy the audience's expectations from the start and prevent complacent observation. The spectator cannot be passive, cannot wait for the story to unfold, cannot give the drama time before mustering up either an intellectual or emotional response. This is not the eye scanning a text; the spectator's seeing already takes place in a strikingly inconsistent space, a space manipulated by surges of spectacle, in which, most important, it becomes increasingly difficult to locate oneself in relation to events on the stage. Because the five visible characters' physical contexts are constantly being challenged and redefined, so are the spectators' contexts. While the spectator is being challenged to look, newly, at every scene, it is her or his proximity to the bodies on the stage that is being challenged. A parallel with film works to some extent; that is, the shifts in spectacle (from light to darkness, from sound to silence) function like a roving camera, manipulating the spectator's physical distance from the events on the stage and, metaphorically, then, the emotional and intellectual distance. Fornes disrupts and manipulates the intensity of the spectator's gaze, disrupts the context, and so highlights the significance of the bodies on the stage as signs and the spectators as interpreters of those signs, a formulation that has special significance for the feminist critic. Fornes is essentially answering Laura Mulvey's plea at the end of her seminal essay "Visual Pleasure and Narrative Cinema" (1975) that we work to disrupt the visual narratives that perpetuate the female's status as the object of an "objective" scrutiny.

Toward this goal Fornes is reworking the relationship between the character as determined by the text and the character as determined by the stage event. A literary assessment of character that would ask questions along the lines of Orlando's motivation in taking Nena as his mistress or explore Leticia's persistent denial of Orlando's political violence in psychological terms would result in a summary of character that the play, in production, resists. The physical, theatrical context for the character's presence in each scene determines its meaning, and so the questions we ask need to be more like, What is the impact of Leticia's sitting while Olimpia mimes her daily routine or the impact of the glimpses we get of Nena's white sleeping gown in the darkness of a scene in which Orlando chases her in the basement? The spectators' sense of characters is determined by the characters', as well as by our own, physical experiences. Our distance from, or proximity to, these bodies as manipulated by spectacle determines our response to these bodies-as-signs by, in essence, drawing us up onto the stage and disorienting us once we are there. Are we with Orlando or Leticia when both are on the stage? Does one perspective dominate another?

Both the characters' and the spectators' roles are being actively structured by text as well as by spectacle. But both are specifically being structured as inconsistent. Although the play opens on Orlando, which may initially seduce the audience into presuming he is the protagonist, the significance of his role in the drama fades as the significance of the women's roles flourishes. As the spectator moves away from the assumption of Orlando's centricity and moves, ideally, toward experiencing protagonists-in-process in Leticia, Olimpia, and Nena, the spectator's role in the production of meaning is increasingly underscored. For the play's goals to be most effectively realized, the spectator must be particularly aware of his or her semiotic role. As Umberto Eco's writings on semiotics stress, theatrical meaning must pass through the spectator. He insists that to a "reacting audience" the mutable body as sign is more complex than language and requires a more attentive and active interpreter (1977, 117). Orlando's career indicates his success at reading those signs; to interrupt his progress the other characters in this drama as well as the spectator need to become comparably authoritative readers of the body as text.

We begin, as of course in the theater we should, by watching. Production of *The Conduct of Life* begins with Orlando doing jumping jacks, the text tells us, "as long as it can be endured" (68). Because the play begins in darkness, and Orlando is already engaged in his exercise routine, the spectator has no way of determining how long he has been at it. The time devoted to the audience's watching this action and hearing nothing but its sounds emphasizes image over content. The spectator is staring and waiting. Crucially, because the image opens the play, it is not yet surrounded by a narrative context; it is more like a painting in a museum than a scene from a play. Like a viewer in a museum who stands before the art surrounded by a personal context—why she is there, whom she is with, why she likes Van Gogh—the spectator has time to forget to look for Fornes's context and to fill the gap with her own. (In a review of the play in the *Nation*, 6 April 1985, Paul Berman writes: "The play conjures a lot of tension, mostly by keeping the scenes tight and disciplined and unsettlingly short. The dialogue and staging seem almost to have been cropped too close at the top or bottom, like those paintings by Philip Pearlstein where the nude's head or leg has been cropped off the edge" [412]. The impact of Pearlstein's work can be precisely in terms of the kind of activity Fornes sets her audience up for—that is, the creative imaging of the body, or any image, we know was complete before the artist performed a reshaping.) To emphasize further the spectator's subjectivity, the subject of the play's opening directions (the "it" being endured) is conspicuously omitted: Is it Orlando's patience and fortitude that is being measured or the spectator's? And, if it is the spectator's endurance, is that endurance being tried by the monotonous image or monotonous noise? At this nascent stage in the drama, Fornes has already established the ambiguity of her subject; she necessitates a critical focus on both Orlando's actions and on the spectator's response to those actions.

When Orlando has finished his routine he begins to speak phrases that ring scripted: "Thirty three and I'm still a lieutenant," he says. "In two years I'll receive a promotion or I'll leave the military." His introduction to himself resonates formally and does not attempt to disguise that it is partially composed in order to convey information to the audience. He continues, "Man must have an ideal, mine is to achieve maximum power" (68), indicating an ominous sense of control over his own career as well as over his language; both his logic and his aspirations seem solid. The audience's perception of Orlando in this opening scene will be controlled by each element of spectacle operating: the light coming up on his jumping jacks; the spotlight that eventually fixes on him; his erect posture in the chair he moves to after he has toweled off; his formal speech.

Orlando sits in the center of the stage, spotlighted, theatrically identified as an actor addressing an audience. Hence, his speech is conveyed as if it were a monologue with acknowledged receivers—in which case, for whom are the jumping jacks? Though the spectator will quickly perceive Orlando's exercise routine as an aspect of his military preparation, it is also an acutely theatrical gesture. Yet the speech is soliloquy insofar as Orlando is alone on the stage and apparently constructing himself *for* himself, rather than for any listener.[1] His formal tone does not entirely disguise the evident personal goal of his speech; he is talking himself into what he wants to become, admitting this his "sexual drive is detrimental to [his] ideals," as if he did not have a judgmental audience. The clouding of the line between monologue and soliloquy begins to prepare the audience for its ensuing work; the spectator is both addressed and ignored, treated as both relevant and irrelevant to the drama's course. Apparently, few assumptions are made about the "character" of the spectator, beyond the assumption that this role is in fact circumscribed by the drama. To an extent the spectator will be responsible for his or her own self-construction, at least in relation to Orlando.

As a character significantly in control of the enacted drama, Orlando's role challenges the spectator to establish him- or herself in either opposition to or support of Orlando's authority and, metaphorically at least, as either independent of or subservient to that authority. Because the play opens with Orlando's strong and commanding voice, the spectator may perceive him as the lens through which she or he will "witness" all ensuing action. Or, to the contrary, are the spectators' moral systems so taken for granted that their condemnation of Orlando is assumed? Though Orlando does admit that he cannot achieve a promotion "on [his] own merit," that he will not let his wife get in the way of his own success, and that he will "eliminate all obstacles," he does so in the context of evident self-knowledge, in the context of admitting to both his strengths and his weaknesses. And, most important, he does so in the *theatrical* context of a man in control both of himself and of the stage space. As the line between the dramatic concepts of monologue and soliloquy were previously obscured, now the line between the play's dramatic and theatrical ideologies is also obscured. His control, at this point in the production, within the theatrical space does much to reinforce his control within the dramatic narrative.

By scene 2 Orlando has achieved his goal: he has become a lieutenant commander. In this sense he has already proved to the spectator the power of his own discourse in the shaping of his reality. He has also proved the power of his theatricality by being transported, in a brief moment of darkness between scenes, from a somewhat desperate aspirant to a man standing in his full army regalia. Though the general spectator has been literally superfluous to Orlando's metamorphosis, spectators internal to the drama have clearly played an active role. In scene 2 Fornes provides the first of a chain of spectators, each of whom will prismatically effect both the characters' and the spectators' perspectives.

The scene opens with Alejo (another lieutenant commander and Orlando and Leticia's "friend," according to the text) sitting at the long dining room table and Orlando and Leticia standing at opposite ends of the large room. In this scene Alejo plays the role of the onlooker, passively seated while Orlando and Leticia pace the room, frequently entering and exiting the stage space. Alejo, veritably mute in context, is not dispensable, however, to the scene's process of meaning. Both Leticia and Orlando address their remarks to Alejo, though they are both undoubtedly speaking for the benefit of the other: "Ask her what she would do if she were rich and could do anything she wants with her money," Orlando directs of Alejo. Leticia responds, without attending Alejo's translation, "I would distribute it among the poor" (69). Both address each other explicitly through Alejo, as Orlando has addressed himself, less explicitly, through the audience in the first scene. Alejo becomes a kind of filter for the scene's meaning; the discourse between Orlando and Leticia is transformed, modified, and stylized for the spectator off the stage.

This verbal transaction between Leticia and Orlando, and the presence of a witness, works like the initial rhyme in a poem; as the rhyme is echoed in later scenes in the play, this primary construct will construe more meaning. Orlando's violent attitude toward Leticia increases rapidly throughout this brief scene, compelling him literally to leave the stage on occasion, presumably to contain himself—or, to hide from his witness. Alejo, though silent, clearly has a power over the progress of this scene; his presence prevents everything but Orlando's emotional violence. When Leticia asserts that she would sacrifice herself to save a deer, "Run in front of the bullets and let the mad hunters kill me . . . stop the bullets with my body," Orlando stomps off the stage, yelling, "You're foolish!—You're foolish! You're a foolish woman!" And when he continues his yelling from offstage, leaving Leticia trying to understand his anger and contempt for her, as well as her own enduring love for him, Alejo's presence seems to have precluded a physically violent situation.

This hint at the larger tableau of consuming violence has, despite Orlando's restraint, a dramatic and theatrical energy that promises ominous and sonorous echoes. The scene's frame, strikingly imbalanced, reinforces that theatrical tension. Leticia begins the discourse with her impassioned and bold argument against hunting, wearing "a dress that suggests 1940s fashion," though it is the present (ca. 1985) and speaking poetically about "the most beautiful animal in the world" (68). She is both romantic and brave. And the scene ends with her similarly romantic question to Alejo, "Do you think I'm crazy? . . . —Because I love him?" (70), now both romantic and insecure. The scene is also framed by Orlando's striking physical presence and then his equally striking absence. Although Orlando's departure leaves Leticia in ostensible control of the stage space, her language denies this; she tells Alejo that she has asked him there to educate her. She announces: "I want to study so I am not an ignorant person. . . . I would like to be a woman who speaks in a group and have others listen" (70). She is not in control of this space, this metaphorical theater within a theater, and Alejo's futile response to her belies this. He asks: "What's the use? . . . Do you think you can change anything?" and looks away from her rather than answering whether she is mad to love Orlando. Above all else the scene has been defined by a disconcerting and tentative stasis—potential energy, though more likely destructive than constructive. Orlando's scarce restraint from physical violence, Alejo's unresponsiveness, and Leticia's spiraling anxiety and unanswered questions all transform the stage space into one in which the significance of events is yet to be determined. Finally, the scene emphasizes what is *not* accomplished through discourse, through speaking and listening.

As if to ensure that the spectator will indeed listen to the silence and gaps as much as to their inversions and opposites, Fornes follows scene 2 with the virtually soundless physical violence of scene 3. The spectator watches Orlando (essentially) rape Nena but first watches an elaborate chase in the very dark warehouse. (The script does not indicate how dark the stage should be, but in the videotaped production I use as my theatrical text in this chapter, from the Billy Rose Collection at the Lincoln Center for the Performing Arts, the stage was so dark in this scene that the spectator had much work to do to make out Orlando's and Nena's movements.)[2] Fornes's stage directions are very specific: *"He grabs her and pushes her against the wall. He pushes his pelvis against her. He moves to the chair dragging her with him. She crawls to the left"* (70), and so on. In production Orlando and Nena move through the steps of this choreography, interrupting their movements with only a line of dialogue each. The spectator's disorientation should be intact; it is difficult to see, there is almost nothing to hear but provocative scuffling, and there is as yet no way to identify Nena. It is also impossible to tell whether Orlando's rape is completed (so to speak), because, as *"he opens his fly and pushes his pelvis against her[,] lights fade to black"* (70). Again, the spectator is left aware, most of all, of what he or she does not know. And in the scene's first echo (sc. 5—imagine an *abab bcbc* rhyme scheme) the spectator's ignorance is further emphasized. Scene 5, in which Orlando searches for Nena, who is hiding in the warehouse, is literally soundless. Both Orlando's and Nena's emotions are unreadable. Nena is motionless and wears a vapid stare; Orlando engages in unexpected restraint: when he finds her, he sits back down in a chair, "staring into space" (73). While they are miming some aspect of a power play, its components remain mysterious.

The positioning of the spectator in relation to the parallel scenes 3 and 5 is complicated, even more by the parallel scenes 4 and 6. To entangle further the series of spectators established through the audience and Alejo, Fornes first devises Leticia as Olimpia's spectator in scene 4 (as Alejo did in sc. 1, Leticia sits still at the long table while Olimpia frantically performs) then provides Leticia with an invisible spectator, Mona, in scene 6. In part, scene 4 provides a kind of

comic relief; Olimpia renders her daily routine for Leticia in almost excruciating detail. The scene can provoke laughter in its nod toward slapstick, as
Olimpia spares us no details:

> I take the top off the milk and pour it in the milk pan except for a little. *(Indi-
> cating with her finger.)* Like this. For the cat. . . . I put coffee in the thing. I
> know how much. . . . I pour the coffee in the coffee pot and the milk in the
> milk pitcher, except I leave *(indicating)* this much for me. (71)

And so on. But Olimpia performs this monologue "in a mumble" and is troubled by a speech defect. So the audience's laughter (as was true at the Theater
for the New City performance cited in my notes) may be nervous and confused;
the spectator should be self-conscious about her or his response.

Leticia's behavior in her temporary role of audience may mimic the general audience's behavior; she appears to be attending direction of some sort. She
is an inattentive spectator who does not get the point. Her response at the end
of Olimpia's lengthy performance is "So?" and Olimpia's "So I need a steam
pot" (71). Insofar as the point of Olimpia's performance was only indirectly to
explain why she needs that particular product, but, more important, to convey
to her mistress the tedium of her daily rituals and to point out to her mistress her
ignorance of that tedium—that is, to make a political point—the performance
has been unproductive. The two women battle for power through a linguistic
game, one that requires Leticia to hear subtext, though she does not. The scene
describes a futile exercise, a virtual waste of language, that ends where it begins,
with Leticia directing Olimpia as spectator, and so keeps both women bound in
the roles their dramatic language prescribes.

In scene 6, scene 4's echo, the audience begins to share more explicitly
with Mona the role of receiver of Leticia's monologues, a sharing burdened
now with both semiotic and political significance: Will the general audience
prove to be more productive spectators than Leticia or Alejo before her?
Mona's ambiguous role—physically absent but imperative for Leticia's self-
expression and change—provokes an exploration of her dramatic and theatrical
status. Later in the play it is established that she may well not actually exist, that
she may be a fiction, which has provocative reverberations for the general spectator's role. Does the playwright or theatrical event engender the audience? If
so, does that necessarily preclude self-determination for that audience? Is the
distinction between literature and theater, or between reader and spectator,
only metaphorical; or is there a genuine political ordeal for the spectator to

undergo? In *Conduct* these issues receive not only theoretical but theatrical regard.

In scene 6 Leticia uses the telephone to describe Orlando's mood changes to Mona and in the process reveals much to the audience about her subservience to him and her fear of extending herself beyond that role. She chronicles their devolving relationship ("I don't know where he goes in his mind. He doesn't listen to me") but conspicuously does not speculate on the nature of Orlando's work. Because Fornes shapes this speech into a monologue rather than a soliloquy, the audience is denied that privileged position of being able to speculate about Leticia's "true" state of mind. We might wonder whether Leticia is as ignorant about the nature of Orlando's work, torturing political prisoners, as she suggests in her lines: "What is there to worry about? Do you think there is anything to worry about?" (74). Or the audience may reasonably presume that Leticia's awareness of an audience, in Mona, in ourselves, may be censoring both her thoughts and speech.

That this monologue begins a scene of remarkable frankness from Alejo—given not only his previous reticence but the more general environment of secrecy—about the impact of Orlando's military torturing on Alejo's sense of self highlights the extent to which Leticia's discourse is dishonest. In addition, the provocative substance of Orlando's speech as he enters the stage with Alejo provides curious reverberations for Leticia's monologue, ones she seems actively *not* to note. Orlando and Alejo enter the scene already talking as Leticia is hanging up the telephone. Orlando's voice, then, merges with Mona's silent offstage voice, in effect completing for the spectator the other side of the discourse not heard. Mona's silence is filled by Orlando's story of two horses mating—a story that describes a sexual encounter in the most violent of sensory terms:

> He made loud sounds not high-pitched like a horse. . . . He was pouring liquid from everywhere, his mouth, his nose, his eyes. He was not a horse but a sexual organ.—Helpless. A viscera—Screaming. Making strange sounds. He collapsed on top of her. (74)

The answer, then, to Leticia's ineffective questioning, her suppression of the knowledge of Orlando's activities, is in the wretched violence of Orlando's depiction of bestial coupling. The horse's articulations—"Screaming. Making strange sounds"—is the bestial response to the subtext of Leticia's monologue: beyond articulation. Orlando inadvertently and indirectly confirms the violent subtext of Leticia's unanswered questions. Leticia, however, chooses to remain deaf; her reaction is no more than this: "Alejo, how are you? Would you like some coffee?" (74).

That the once mute and cynical spectator in Alejo now becomes an honest and responsive critic furthers the spectator's preparation for an active encounter with this theatrical event. To Orlando's "What is viciousness?" Alejo can now respond, "You." Orlando's violence has enervated Alejo through its momentum. "I didn't know anyone could behave the way you did," he says, referring to Orlando's torturing of a political prisoner: "It frightened me. It changed me. I became hopeless" (75). But, when Alejo seeks to spur Leticia to honesty, he is unsuccessful. He turns to her to say: "I have no feelings. . . . I'm impotent," though she does not, in turn, embrace the responsible spectator's role. She refuses, still, to seek the truth. "Nonsense," she replies (76).

The play is beginning to shift toward Leticia as its most important agent. Her failure as a spectator—her failure at being an active reader of the various "texts" surrounding her—begins to direct the movement of the drama as a whole. After another brief scene (sc. 7) imaging Orlando's violation of Nena (a scene meant to recall the viewer from Orlando's torturing of prisoners to Orlando's violence within the home), Leticia and Olimpia enact a scene in which Olimpia tries to be a responsible spectator (reader, critic), even if it is, ironically, only through acting. But her efforts go thoroughly unappreciated by Leticia. Though Olimpia pretends to be able to read in order to help Leticia memorize a passage from a text, Leticia responds only with anger and violence: *"(Slapping the book off Olimpia's hand.)* Why are you pretending you can read?" (76–77). Leticia plays both the actor disrespectful of her relationship to the audience as well as the spectator unwilling to pry into the course of events (her question to Olimpia is rhetorical at best). The striking shift toward physical violence—really, the imaging of this particular relationship by the violence between these two characters, ironically between these two women rather than between Orlando and Leticia, for example—is what begins to highlight here the moral component of the spectator's role. As a witness to Orlando's violence (at the very least, Leticia can hear his violence toward Nena), she is only mimicking his behavior rather than urging change or defying its impact.

Scenes 11 and 12 begin a restructuring of the drama that will peak in scene 15. Olimpia becomes a more pivotal presence, in scene 13 bold enough to describe Orlando as "like an alligator, big mouth and no brains. Lots of teeth but no brains. All tongue" (79), as her own and Leticia's roles as listeners are further explored. Fornes describes what constitutes an audience—who the spectator is, what roles he or she might play—through a contrast of Olimpia and Leticia. In scene 11 the audience witnesses Olimpia play a part that both mimics

Leticia and bests her. Olimpia now becomes violent; she hits Orlando, tries to strangle him, even threatens castration. She does so over the issue of his treatment of Nena, over that particular violence that echoes the paradigm of his greater violence. But Olimpia reveals an awareness of her power as a spectator that Leticia has yet to realize. First, Olimpia knows that Nena is watching her and recognizes that this makes her directly responsible to Nena. She takes the time to turn to Nena and say, "You're pretty" (81), even if her words are almost lost in the scene's furious, emotional violence. Moreover, she has directly confronted that actor who has, so far, been most central, the man in control of this theatrical space.

The nature of her exchange with Orlando suggests that Olimpia, despite her servant status, is not powerless, even in Orlando's home. To her "One day I'm going to kill you when you're asleep," Orlando responds, "I'm getting rid of you too!" (80), a less than purely masterful response. By the end of the scene Orlando is ranting, shouting his hate to Olimpia as well as to Alejo (who has sat silently throughout the scene), trying desperately to dismiss his audience. Olimpia has essentially compelled him to look back out into the darkness, out into the audience, in order to recognize the complexity of his own role, and there are tangible results; in his next scene Orlando tries to explain his treatment of Nena to Nena, and, though his words are hardly palatable, they are at least exploratory:

> What I do to you is out of love. Out of want. It's not what you think. I wish you didn't have to be hurt. . . . It is quiet and it pierces my insides in the most internal way. It is my most private self. And this I give to you. . . . —It is a desire to destroy and to see things destroyed and to see the inside of them.— It's my nature. . . . —I need love. I wish you did not feel hurt and recoil from me. (82)

Orlando is trying to justify himself to his audience.

Olimpia's boldness in scene 11 is followed in scene 12 initially by Leticia's continued denial but then by something that also verges on boldness. Critically, this scene is framed by another discussion between Leticia and Mona, though this time the deconstruction of the very notion of a privileged audience—and, hence, of a unified audience—is explicit: Leticia begins the scene alone on the stage, next to the telephone but speaking to Mona only "in her mind." Now Leticia tells her audience that she knows Orlando is keeping someone in their basement, though she still elaborates, "I don't dare look." After a pause she responds to an imaginary question: "No, there's nothing I can do. I can't do anything." Though to some extent Leticia begins to articulate the complexity of her emotional response—jealousy, anger, fear—by imagining a receiver for her expression, she is still using the idea of a receiver as a means toward denial. The honesty and integrity of her response is significantly obscured for the general spectator by Leticia's need to create that receiver. At the very least Leticia is attempting to pass responsibility to Mona or to any other spectator. But something about Leticia's "exchange" with Mona in this scene empowers her. The possibility of an audience, of being listened to, provides the impetus at this point for action. By the scene's end Leticia becomes emboldened; she announces: "I'm going down [to the cellar]. I want to see who is there" (81).

The theatrical issue is: What role has the spectator, either Mona or the general audience, played in this emboldening? The never-seen Mona's role extends the dramatic world of *Conduct* out into an unseen space: the audience's space. Though the audience can have no real impact on the scripted drama, the play suggests that in a broader sense—metaphorically, at the very least—audience in general has enormous impact on the course of events. Whether Mona is real or fictive becomes an important question for the spectator. To what extent is she necessary to Leticia; to what extent does audience engender action, good or bad? Mona is not the only character threatened with erasure here; the spectator's character is similarly vulnerable. At this point the drama literally requires the spectator's active participation, morally if not theatrically. Dramatically, Leticia acknowledges the importance of the spectator by expressing her need for Mona; in scene 14, when Leticia has finally confronted Orlando (if somewhat pathetically), though she does not insist on Nena's leaving, she does insist on Mona's coming. Leticia would like to bring Mona—bring the spectator—into this particular stage space. The spectator's presence has become crucial to Leticia in terms of her own characterization as an actor. The spectator completes her.

Olimpia and Nena have an actor/spectator relationship themselves, which does not require the lassoing of another spectator like Mona. The servant and child have a relationship that transcends the other relationships in the play in its productivity: Olimpia is Nena's sympathetic, morally conscious spectator/listener. In scene 15 the woman and child are seated side by side, balanced within the entire scene's spectacle, while Nena narrates her history with Olimpia's encouragement. In production the scene is arrestingly longer than any other scene and strikingly less frenetic. The two women calmly and methodically separate stones from dried beans, even while Nena describes her tragic and brutal life before, during, and since Orlando's abduction of her.

Nena's opening words reveal that the two women have been engaged in discourse before. "I used to clean beans when I was in the home," Nena says, continuing a story that the audience has not heard but Olimpia clearly has. Nena makes explicit Olimpia's role in relation to herself: "Since my ma died there just wasn't anyone watching over me. Except you. . . . I am glad to be here because you are here." Initially, Nena's discourse describes her own desire to watch over her grandfather as Olimpia has been watching over Nena. Just as Olimpia cannot protect Nena from Orlando's abuse, Nena knows she cannot protect her grandfather from the abuses inherent to living in the street. But Nena could keep her grandfather's box clean, dry, and warm, and she could use her own body to ease her grandfather's discomfort by letting him sleep on top of her and by watching over him as he sleeps. Being watched over takes on special emphasis for Nena. She asserts, "You can't sleep . . . not if there isn't someone watching over you while you sleep," which prefaces her acknowledgment that Olimpia has been watching over her. The spectator, Nena suggests, can be genuinely helpful. Even Orlando's abuse of her has changed since he brought her to the house. He used to keep Nena elsewhere: "And sometimes he brought me food and sometimes he didn't. . . . And he hung me on the wall," but now, with potential spectators in the house ("I am glad to be here because you are here"), "he doesn't beat me so much anymore" (84).

Olimpia and Nena's discussion has enabled two critical movements for Nena, both the expression of her worst pain and the desire, and conceivably the ability, to surmount the experience. Nena describes for Olimpia the details of Orlando's sexual abuse and intimates by silence the ensuing threat of a complete loss of self:

> And he puts his hand on me and he recites poetry. He touches himself and he touches his stomach and his breasts and his behind. He puts his fingers in my parts and he keeps reciting. Then he turns me on my stomach and puts himself inside me. And he says I belong to him.

Stage directions indicate that a pause follows this last line, the first pause since Nena has begun her story, a flowing discourse of phrases, each beginning with *And.* Now she pauses at this moment when she has articulated the worst threat to her self, to conclude: "I want to conduct each day of my life in the best possible way." With Olimpia beside her Nena says: "I should value all those who are near me. And I should value the kindness that others bestow upon me." She is actively appreciating Olimpia's productive role as her personal, attentive audience. And she promises to become that kind of spectator in turn. "And if someone should treat me unkindly," she says, "I should not blind myself with rage, but I should see them and receive them, since maybe they are in worse pain than me" (85). By being a responsive witness, and by seeing that role reflected in Olimpia, Nena is essentially saved.

Though Leticia is not witness to this perfect transaction between actor and spectator, the next scene juxtaposes her movement toward a better understanding of what her role has been in relation to Orlando all these years. She has been his spectator since he was a child, and now that role has become ominous. Though Leticia is still not entirely willing to accept her responsibility—that is, to accept the truth about Orlando's activities and how her inability or unwillingness to challenge him allows their perpetuation—she is beginning to see its larger reverberations. On the telephone with Mona, Leticia occasions a more explicit delineation of Orlando's operations: "He tortures people. I know he does. . . . Sometimes he comes from headquarters and his hands are shaking." Though she says that Orlando denies this, she insists that "everybody knows it." She moves beyond Orlando and herself to describe the entire nation's place in these tortures:

> Sometimes you see blood in the streets. . . . Why do they leave the bodies in the street . . . to frighten people? They tear their fingernails off and their poor hands are bloody and destroyed. And they mangle their genitals and expose them and they tear their eyes out and you can see the empty eyesockets in the skull. (85)

The irony of her own depiction of these events apparently eludes Leticia for the time being. The villains virtually compel the innocent into the role of spectator, offering them information enough not only to frighten but to infuriate. But they also "tear their eyes out," prevent vision for both the victims and the witnesses; the terror becomes a terror of *seeing*. Unlike Nena, Leticia cannot therefore imagine her role as potentially productive. If she truly sees, she suggests, she will become impotent, as Alejo did. Hence, she only tells Mona, which may not be telling anyone at all; she still ensures her distance from these events and, in turn, need not embrace her responsibility to others.

The next scene is conspicuous both for its brevity and its shift of politics. Leticia enters the room as Olimpia engages in apparently irrelevant talk with Nena about high-heeled shoes, ingrown nails, her mother's blood sugar, and glaucoma. Contextualized by the violence of all its surrounding scenes, the scene attracts special attention. The three women end up sitting together at the same table, all looking out toward the audience. Leticia asks, "So, what are you talking about?" to which Olimpia responds, "Ingrown nails" (86). This is the first time Leticia and Nena have been onstage together, and it is unremarkable; the stage space is not transformed into the violent space one might anticipate. To the contrary, it is three women talking, self-absorbedly but uneventfully. Leticia seems to be approaching the world of Olimpia and Nena: as much as she allows Nena to stay in the room, Olimpia and Nena stay and allow Leticia to participate in their conversation. The presence of three women on the stage, and their women-centered discourse, marks the scene as transitional, the shift in tone as dramatic.

The final scene begins with the two dominant actors acknowledging that they are onstage. "Talk," Orlando commands Leticia. "I can't talk like this," she responds. "In front of everyone. It is personal. I don't need the whole world to know" (86–87). "Everyone" would have to refer to Orlando, Olimpia, and Nena. But the audience knows that, if anyone has secrets at this point in the drama, it will not be any of the women but, instead, Orlando. Leticia's "everyone," then, is her larger audience. Leticia is still unable to tell the truth for this audience, partially because Orlando prevents it. He will not allow his story to be told to the "whole world." He therefore forces Leticia to collaborate with him in constructing a fiction. But one wonders whom they are saving from the truth. Within their dramatic world the truth is evident, and its obscuring only sustains the status quo that is no longer palatable or possible, for that matter, for either of them. The play, their play, then, is protecting the theater audience from the truth. What would the audience be morally required to do, the play indirectly asks, if they knew the truth?

Orlando now accosts Leticia with physical violence—he grabs her hair, while Nena hides her face. Orlando imposes a narrative on Leticia; he wants to believe that she has a lover, presumably so that he can justify his violence. And, in order, ironically, to waylay that violence, Leticia narrates an imaginary affair with Orlando's prompting. Their confrontation is purely dishonest, obviously enacted for the sake of the audience rather than for the sake of any resolution between the two characters. This is metatheater at its finest; the two consciously engage in theatrical production, playing fully the role of actors but with no pretense toward the truth.

If nothing else to this point has been entirely successful at awakening Leticia, this exercise finally makes her aware of her entire audience. Forced to both "act out" in Orlando's drama and to be her own spectator within that drama, she is forced in turn to acknowledge that it takes both actor and audience to perpetuate the delusions, as she and Orlando are so thoroughly engaged in doing. Leticia's solution is to kill the primary actors in this drama then to leave her spectators, worthy or not, to their own devices. She shoots Orlando and asks Nena to shoot her in turn.[3]

Everyone within this drama plays the role of spectator; everyone is witness to some violence and altered by that witnessing. Orlando, however, at the head of the chain in this particular paradigm, is the only one annihilated by the violence. Fornes does not offer closure to the women's stories, as she does to the men's. Guiltless, though, they are not. While Nena is the consummate victim of what both Leticia and Olimpia are also victims of—that is, that violence perpetuated by a "masculine" society—Leticia and Olimpia are also guilty of perpetuating that violence through their various stages of denial, through futile anger, and in their own master-subject relationship. But scenes 15 and 17 (Nena's narrative and the three women's roundtable scene) have illustrated a potential movement for them beyond that relationship, a movement toward a "feminine" world of nonviolence.

By the final scene Leticia herself becomes an object for Orlando's physical violence, as she has been an object for his emotional violence throughout the play. Finally, she becomes the literal perpetrator of physical violence when she murders Orlando. She has been—allowed herself to be?—co-opted into the system. And perhaps most disturbing is the play's ending on her mute plea to Nena to murder her, that is, her plea to Nena to engage in the violence herself. Leticia has internalized the system of violence that has co-opted her to such an extent that she becomes, like Shakespeare's Othello, both victim and victimizer, both actor and spectator. But, unlike Othello, Leticia does not succeed in providing closure to her own story. And both Nena and Olimpia will survive these stage events. Through their status Fornes communicates a remarkable message of hope, tentative as it is: the violence may no longer be perpetuated. The spectator in the audience who can visualize his or her role as parallel to Olimpia's, or even Nena's, rather than Mona's or Alejo's, can become accomplice not as the spectator of Latin American violence is but, rather, as Olimpia is an accomplice in the redemption of Nena or as both Olimpia and Nena may be in the redemption of Leticia. The spectator needs to recognize him- or herself as actor as well.

The play's set accentuates the increasing focus on the women characters. The stage space has been increasingly dominated by women throughout the drama; by the end it is entirely their space. Throughout, the women's interactions have echoed and reflected one another's actions, while Orlando has seemed to be occupying a different stage space. He has, in fact, literally occupied a space in which neither Leticia nor Olimpia has tread throughout the course of the play (at least, not before the eyes of the spectators). W. B. Worthen offers a helpful reading of certain elements of spectacle, particularly set design, in the process of meaning in *Conduct:*

> [The play] uses the disposition of the stage to reflect and extend [the] vision of social corruption. . . . The set provides a visual emblem of the hierarchy of power in the play. More significantly, though, the set constructs a powerful habit of vision for the spectators. The living and dining rooms—those areas of public sociability where Olimpia serves coffee, Leticia and Orlando discuss their marriage, Olimpia and Nena gossip while preparing dinner—become transparent to the audience as windows into the upstage sets [the house's cellar and warehouse] and the occluded "setting" they represent: the warehouse and basements where the real life of this society—torture, rape, betrayal—is conducted. (174–75)

Precisely because of both the very different and similar natures of the events that transpire within the different locations of the constructed set, the impact of the set should not be underestimated. Worthen describes here how this space dramatically and theatrically realizes the theme of violent reverberations. The concept of the downstage set functioning as a window to the upstage set is very persuasive and also highlights the spectator's role as viewer.

Those strengths noted, I find Worthen's reading a little too literal. Why is the "real life," in Worthen's term, that aspect of the life of this drama controlled by the prominent male? Part of the problem lies in Worthen's characterization of the events that transpire within these spaces. He refers to the discourse between Olimpia and Nena as "gossip," for which I find no evidence. Nor do I hear Orlando and Leticia "discuss their marriage." And Worthen locates the concepts of "torture, rape, and betrayal" within that inner space of the warehouse and basement, at least two of which are as dominant in the downstage space. To the contrary, the foregrounding of what Worthen refers to as the "social" spaces provides not only a window but also a different figuring of similar space.

The deceptive simplicity of the stage space in *The Conduct of Life* underscores the critical process of the destabilization of both the spectators' and characters' roles. Contrary to what one might expect, in the text Fornes describes a multiplatformed space that translates on the stage into levels that curiously locate the basement above and behind the living and dining rooms. This physical inversion has both theatrical and political consequences. The hierarchy of the spaces and the actions and concepts they house are undermined. Placing the basement, the male-dominated space within this drama, both above and behind the dining room, the female-dominated space, results in equalizing the impact of each.

The foregrounded space, the living and dining rooms, is the space of discourse throughout the drama and eventually becomes the primary space of discourse, betrayal, and physical and emotional torture. It is a space markedly affected by both dramatic and theatrical change throughout production. As the drama progresses, the foregrounded space bears increasingly the burden of activity; by the final scene the stage is "reduced" to that space. All political and theatrical action is contextualized by that "social" space.

The predominance of female characters, female voices, and female bodies peaks in the final scene, when the central male is murdered. The stage becomes the women's stage, as Leticia had nearly prophesied, despite her efforts to play the deer, to put her body before the sighted gun. To this point in the drama each character (with the exception of Alejo and, of course, Mona) has verbally and physically interacted with every other character. But by the play's end the male characters have been removed, and it is the women's consciousness that pervades the stage. And, as throughout the play the audience has witnessed only the female body as the recipient of violence (only hearing about violence to the male body), the stage now becomes an extension of the representation of that female body.

At critical moments in the drama both Nena's voice and body encompass the female voice and body in this play; again, she is the consummate victim to what both Olimpia and Leticia are also victims. Nena is also the consummate "character" in this theatrical drama, quintessential actor and spectator, most physically active on the stage, likely listened to most attentively (in sc. 15), and in the final scene asked to play the roles of actor and spectator simultaneously— to take on the responsibility of both those roles when Leticia hands her the gun and asks, essentially, that, as witness to these events, Nena act. Rather than embrace a response to this play like Worthen's that locates Orlando as the instigator of all action, or protagonist, I consider Nena the eye of this drama. To recognize a character as an eye, or focus, is to undermine a linear, causal reading and to provide, instead, a reading that moves out from the center.

The complexities of echoing scenes and echoing spaces in *Conduct* partially preclude a linear plotting of causal relationships between characters and their actions. Violence is finally a kind of web in this play; it engenders not forward movement but outward movement and ensnares all the characters in a network of role-playing. This network, which can be broken down to a network of spectators, is tangled by Mona's invisibility. Since the audience cannot evaluate Mona beyond her causal relationship with Leticia, she becomes a gap that must be reckoned with as a gap. Her role in this drama is determined by her literal absence, which is what finally most explicitly extends this drama out into the audience's space, where they too are absent from the drama.

I think that Fornes prescribes a woman as the play's constructed spectator.[4] An approach to the play's structure that de-emphasizes the linear in favor of the indeterminably shaped but powerful structure of a web undermines the concept of protagonist. For Fornes *antagonist* and *protagonist* become suspect terms. Efforts by individual characters to use other characters throughout the play do not distinguish the user but, rather, connect him or her inextricably with the other characters. The play describes a continuous pulling-in of characters into the center: none of their actions is innocuous; they are never free of one another, never spared any impact of another's activity. But, again, the play increasingly focuses on the female characters. The stage is initially dominated by women and eventually inhabited only by women. Their actions on the stage are so utterly interconnected, constantly echoed and reflected among them, up to the moment of profound ambiguity about agency at the play's end, that one may assert that they are, in their combined consciousness, a single theatrical force. As Fornes explores in so many of her plays, action is about interaction, and by this play's end it is specifically about women's interaction.

Fornes's ideal spectator for this play is a woman because, as an *active* spectator, she will find herself echoed within the play's own internal echoes. Despite Orlando's one opportunity to be a spectator in the final scene, he declines the role, acts only as author and director, and is killed off. By his own admission the impact of Alejo's role as spectator was also a kind of death. And, although Leticia shoots Orlando and extends the gun to Nena with the silent invitation that Nena shoot her, I will go so far as to say she will not, because, even though Fornes provides no such closure, Nena has cumulatively learned the moral responsibility of the spectator. She knows the power inherent in that role.

Insofar as Mona is a kind of silent echo, or invisible mirror, for the other female characters in this drama, she may have the same relationship to the play's external female spectator. Symbiotic as the connections between the female characters are in this drama, Mona, as noted, represents a gap. In this context the woman in the audience may be the one to fill that gap, the implicit link in the chain. Because at least Olimpia and Nena survive the violence of this dramatic world, and because Leticia may well survive it too, the dramatic and linguistic relationships between these women have particular resonance. And the circle is far from closed. Scenes 15 and 17 demand an echo from scene 19, the final scene in the play. Though it does not happen within the course of this drama, this dramatic space needs to be claimed as the women's space—and the play's structure as both a series of rhymes and a web promises the possibility of this achievement.

The spectator, and perhaps explicitly the feminist spectator, should see this drama as coiled and recognize the need to loop back before looking forward. Olimpia and Nena, at least, can start that coil forward again. (It may be that, in Leticia's request to Nena that she shoot her, Leticia is offering to take on the burden of Nena's victimization, which will then die with her.) But, at the risk of undermining the argument laid out here, it would be misleading to insist on either of the play's possible endings, that is, in the death or survival of Leticia. It is in the uncertainty of Leticia's fate that Fornes's drama parallels some of the most important feminist theater of the past decade. The most significant moral component of the spectator's role emerges in that moment of lack of closure. As Sharon Willis explains in her essay "Hélène Cixous's *Le Portrait de Dora:* The Unseen and the Un-Scene" (1990), for example, in the context of an unseen conclusion "the menace of closure persists" (90). In that menacing moment the spectator needs to recognize her impact, her role in the production of meaning up to and beyond this point. Lack of closure, Willis elaborates, "opens and closes a distance—between voice and body, eye and ear, speech and listener/spectator"—and within that particular mise-en-scène the spectator should recognize her profoundly ambiguous distance from the body as spectacle and see herself on the stage, "mapped there" (91).

Painful and tragic as both the process and "conclusion" of this play are, Fornes keeps the closure unclosed, the theatrical stage a place for an as yet unnamed progress. She effectively turns the table on the spectator, suggesting that closure is not achieved both within and beyond the drama—and will not be at least until the spectator realizes the moral responsibility of that role. Too many elements of the theater are taken for granted, Fornes implies, that is, that the text determines the character, that the power hierarchy runs from playwright to director to character to spectator. Fornes's plays rebel from these formulations first by underscoring them, by delineating each of those roles in operation, and then by illustrating how the text can be affected by the theater, how spectacle can define a character, and how spectacle can position the spectator. Character, like the self more generally, is always in flux; the process of representing character via text alone is, therefore, inherently untrustworthy. Fornes has dealt with this challenge to representation over the years by foregrounding sensual and sexual relationships between characters. She overlays images of characters *enacting* their desires while they struggle for power over the otherwise suspiciously fixed literary text.

6

Palimpsests

The theater dramatizes, makes perceptible, literary themes; concepts are made visual; they exist—as they do in life—in both language and the image. We do not only hear about abuse, for example, we can see it; we see Orlando's molestation of Nena. There is no opportunity in the theater for the spectator to forget context either for thought or for action; we cannot forget that Shakespeare's Othello is a Moor surrounded by Caucasians or that Hamlet is forced to see Claudius actually sit on his father's throne. Like the self more generally, the theatrical character is defined by context, by whom as well as what it comes up against. Chekhov made certain to keep the spectators' gaze on the cherry orchard, whose branches brush the stage space, in order to give us more insight into the characters' contentions with the past. The orchard is an image of that past, and, as the characters enact their conflicts in the very context of what has compelled those conflicts, their struggles become more than abstraction.

In this chapter I explore the theatrical palimpsest in Fornes's theater, the simultaneous literary and visual texts that *are* theater. Fornes has with increasing care highlighted the palimpsestic nature of the theater, particularly to illuminate the functioning and intersection of her characters' labors for power and the realization of their desires.

Her characters are frequently sexual, always sensual and emotional, always physical. For thirty years Fornes has complemented each of her character's intelligence with his or her sensuality. That meaning invoked by what characters say to one another is mediated by what the spectator sees the characters do to one another as they act out their sensuality. Her characterizations become more unstable and more authentic simultaneously; through the imaging of characters' desires, we see how the self can be simultaneously powerful and powerless, how desire can be simultaneously punishing and enabling.

Typical of Fornes's dichotomies, desire makes her characters impervious and vulnerable simultaneously. It is both selfish and necessary, punishing and rewarding to the self and to the other, central to the complex and ambiguous tasks of attaining subjectivity and objectivity. Desire formulates the subject and necessarily engenders an object, but its obscuring of boundaries threatens the integrity of both the lover and the beloved in Fornes's plays, even while it contributes to their sense of completion.

Within individual plays and within her oeuvre, a haunting lyricism results from the patterns that emerge when characters act out their desires in struggles for power over themselves and one another. The history of Fornes's theater has been, in fact, a history of representing that desire and its complicated web of simultaneous targets and aspirations: the achievement of a self, the procuring of a lover, the forging of a satisfactory role within a community—each of which act violently disrupts the self and the other.

Fornes has been consistently devoted to relationships as the most productive narrative context for the representation of what it is to be human. She has been consistently devoted, too, to the body as the site of that drama, which lends a particularly sensual quality to her stages, obscuring a line between mere physicality and sexuality. In the tradition of sensual writers like Anais Nin, Fornes uses physicality to explore some of the less tangible, more elusive connections between people. She often substitutes exposition and psychology with the equally telling image. As Ross Wetzsteon suggests, "Fornes's heart doesn't seem to be in psychologizing, she seems to use it only to *depsychologize* the scene, she's much more comfortable explaining to the actress how she wants her to sit down—that's the kind of grounding she focuses on" (1986, 43). The subtleties of characters' relationships are often defined by physical gestures, ranging from pouring bourbon and bringing soup in *Fefu* to the exhibitionist masturbation in *Mud* to explicit sexual foreplay in *Sarita*. Characters are always undergoing a process of definition through their physical interactions with others. Whether explicitly sexual or not, these interactions are profoundly intimate and symbolic of desire.

Fornes's characters have internalized the theater, watching themselves and one another as if they were watching performances. Their sensuality, in turn, takes on highly theatrical attributes; sensuality is projected outward into the image of the character: the spectator *sees* that sensuality in order to comprehend characters' words and actions. In this chapter I read moments of simultaneous texts—the narrative and the image—in the four plays discussed in the preceding chapters, as well as in *Abingdon Square* (1987) and in *What of the Night?* (1993), in order to explore character often as the result of the convergence of the literary and imagistic texts of desire and power.

Within the theatrical world of *Fefu and Her Friends* the relationships that matter most are the relationships the spectator sees. The visual text subsumes the supposed social and cultural text of "a man's world." The omission of men from *Fefu*, particularly when considered in light of Fornes's thematic and formal scope over thirty or so years, may be directly responsible for any empowerment of its women. The women are allowed to recreate their relationships—for that matter, they are allowed to have relationships—without the mediation of a *Conduct of Life*'s Orlando, for example. The palimpsest of the women's interactive presences over their tortured narratives of oppression, fear, and anger offers the women redemption. The space for desire ultimately unmediated by men often allows for that desire's productivity.

In *Fefu* characters are largely defined by their desires, and whatever *images* of desire— sexual or otherwise—Fornes provides are between women. Men are referred to, particularly Fefu's husband, Phillip, but they remain beyond the audience's field of vision. Therefore, though heterosexual desire makes it into the dramatic text, it does not make it into the theatrical text. Even when the topics of the women's conversations cover characters, real or imaginary, outside of their theatrical event, their concerns are with themselves and one another above all else. Their desires, as imaged in this theatrical event, are for the comfort and support of the women with whom they share this space. And those desires are responded to.

Fefu's other desire, ostensibly for her husband, is both punishing and enabling. She experiences her desire for Phillip as ultimately damaging to her autonomy. But that desire is finally proxy for a desire for her own self's health. In the play's last act Fefu tells Julia that Phillip has left her:

> His body is here but the rest is gone. . . . I torment him and I torment myself. I need him, Julia. . . . I need his touch. . . . I need the person he is. I can't give him up. *(She looks into Julia's eyes.)* I look into your eyes and I know what you see. It's death. Fight! (139–40)

The irony of "His body is here"—when his body is not here—foregrounds the productive possibilities of even unmet desire in Fefu's experience. Fefu imagines that Julia sees her need for Phillip as a kind of "death" to herself, but, to the contrary, she implies, it saves her. It is not Phillip who can save her but the desire for Phillip; "his body is gone," but Fefu does not finally need his body on this stage in order to experience her own desire—which is a way of avoiding the death that has been the consequence of Julia's eradication of her own capacity to desire.

In *Mud, Abingdon Square,* and *Sarita* Fornes concerns herself with the components of a woman's desire—how desire is constructed as both self-nurturing and as defense against persecution. Fornes increasingly explores women's characters in her later work: *The Successful Life of 3's* lackadaisical She makes way for *Mud's* rebellious Mae; the romantic Molly of *Molly's Dream* makes way for the sexually and emotionally complex heroine of *Sarita*. Acting out desire becomes largely responsible for the producing of a woman's role, sometimes against societal expectations.

Mud depicts Mae's thwarted desires for a realized self in the image of the voyeuristic sex imposed upon her by Henry and Lloyd. At separate moments in the drama both Lloyd and Henry masturbate in front of Mae. Though both insist that they do so in efforts to compel Mae to make love to them—that is, in an inverted process of lovemaking or seduction—both are in fact putting on performances that Mae is compelled to watch. Their masturbations are meant to master Mae by forcing her into the position of voyeur, unwittingly and unwillingly included in their sexual acts; she is necessary for the masturbator's climax. While Mae's verbal exchanges with Henry and Lloyd *say* that all of their behavior results from the frustrations of poverty, ignorance, inability to communicate, and unfulfilled needs—or even from Mae's manipulations as she aggressively seeks power—the theatrical image of the men's masturbations demonstrates that the men prevent the possibility for Mae of productive "intercourse."

Lloyd and Henry's supposed desire for Mae is punishing for all the characters in the constrained dramatic world of *Mud.* Unexamined and fettered, that desire is never realized as a desire for their own autonomy; repressed, it then violently reemerges as a coveting of Mae, which, in an effort to prevent her from leaving the stage, compels Lloyd to kill her, leaving him and Henry bereft. Mae's desire is subject to these same constraints; her repressed desires reemerge purely selfishly as a desire to improve herself but with no awareness of the need to alter context to do so. For Mae, however, her desire is enabling as well: she becomes a poet and achieves self-love, even if only at the moment of her death—though the visual palimpsest offers no cause for celebration. Her dead and bloody body eclipses anything that has been productive about her desire.

Marion of *Abingdon Square* resembles Mae, though in a completely different world, a world of wealth and privilege, a genuinely beautiful world not of a dark kitchen embedded in mud but of space and light, of French doors and gardens. Her dramatic life begins as pure romance, her much older husband-to-be, Justin, singing Handel to her, her husband's son Michael her dancing partner and friend. But Marion, like Mae, feels crippled by her ignorance. Her education was interrupted by the death of her parents, and she feels she does not "yet comprehend a great many things" (6). That assessment is followed by a scene in which she and her cousin Mary muse upon the sexual lives of others and are then consumed with guilt. Marion seeks to use her self-education as punishment for that guilt; she studies Dante's "Purgatorio" by standing painfully in her overheated attic, "on her toes with her arms outstretched, looking upward" (11). Her self-education is excruciating. She explains to her great-aunt Millie, who finds her in this posture:

> I feel sometimes that I am drowning in vagueness—that I have no character.
> . . . I do this to strengthen my mind and my body. I am trying to conquer this
> vagueness I have inside of me. This lack of character. . . . This weakness. (13)

Marion constructs her own palimpsest; she essays to offer up an image of herself as strong in contrast to her profound experience of weakness.

Eventually, Marion extends her search for self-definition into a blatant using of men. When her books and religion do not work, Marion becomes a writer of sorts, keeping a daily "diary," which is really a fictional revisioning of her life. She writes in a lover, a mysterious man with the first initial *F,* who does in fact enter her life through the streets of New York's West Village and eventually through her husband's French doors. But even then he is not the lover she initially takes. Marion protects herself from an actual lover by taking instead the house painter (their one sexual encounter leads to the conception of her child). Terror of her own sexual desire and the subsequent indication of a powerful and dangerous self to Marion necessitate the continuation of the self-denying pattern begun with marrying a much older man, to whom Marion feels indebted but not in love. In time, something like courage, but more like need, compels her to live her devised fiction. Frank becomes her lover, and she even relocates herself into another space, into an apartment for "privacy" on Abingdon Square.

Despite Marion's increasing aggression, these are futile steps to alter a resolute context, which is that of a young, orphaned woman, insufficiently educated, fettered by marriage, controlled by the men who benignly enough are the masters of that context. Marion finally becomes motivated by what is figured as sexual desire above all else, eventually depicted as destructive. Inevitably, it destroys her marriage to Justin and hence terminates her companionship with Michael, who insists he must remain faithful to his father. Frank acts the typically elusive lover, who insists they must be careful and so distances himself from her. Marion had hoped through her fiction to become alive, to live her own life, but she experiences the consequences of that vitality as threatening even to that unrealized self: "When I sinned against life because I was dead I was not punished," she insists. "Now that life has entered me I am destroyed and I destroy everything around me" (34).

Fulfilling the prophecy of the larger script in which she acts—that is, the script that defines her as a young wife, inherently and futilely rebellious—Marion becomes a menacing sexual animal, at least according to Justin. After their separation he tells Michael:

> Last week I followed her to a dance parlor. . . . Marion's behavior is irrational. She's not sane. . . . I followed her in and I took a table by the window. A man wearing a soldier's uniform greeted her. They started dancing. And moved to a dark corner. She knew I was there looking at her and that's why she did what she did. They kissed and caressed lewdly. I've never seen such behavior in public. (35)

Marion accepts Justin's definition of her. She describes to Mary her instinct to murder Justin by shooting him, which would give her "a great satisfaction. A satisfaction equal to flushing a toilet. . . . I am crude. I know I'm crude. I know I'm uncivilized" (36). Though Marion is essentially humbled and prostrate at Justin's bedside as he is likely to die from a stroke, the drama holds her responsible for his death: her lifelong repression engendered a violence that fell over into all of their lives (Justin's stroke was the consequence of a scene in which the two stood facing each other with guns). With great and sad irony, Marion becomes the abuser as the consequence of the abuse of a world that gave her no room for self-definition; she is an agent only when acting *against* others, imaged via her instigated sexual encounters, each of which tell the story of a woman reduced to a kind of physical hysteria in efforts to achieve a self.

The eponymous protagonist of *Sarita* is one of the only female characters Fornes's audience actually sees making love. But when Sarita makes love— either physically with Julio or verbally with Mark—she is not giving love or sex as much as taking her own satisfaction. Sarita is empowered by her impulses toward self-fulfillment. While Fornes celebrates Sarita's sexuality, particularly by contrasting her with her mother, Fela, who has effectively been deadened by her passionless life, she also suggests that Sarita's desire is what causes her tragedy. Sarita is so consumed with desire for Julio that she has sex with him repeatedly at the cost of both her self-esteem and her marriage with Mark. Ironically, it is Julio who clarifies Sarita's conduct; he eventually asks her for money, confirming that he has been playing her prostitute.

Although Sarita never comes to the realization, Fornes illustrates that Sarita's desire for Julio has been misdirected from the start. Sarita's real desire, projected onto Julio and contextualized by an affair, has been for her own self. As discussed in chapter 4, Fornes spends considerable time imaging Sarita in the act of making love. Those images, when viewed through the lens of Fornes's appreciation of Sarita's sexuality, suggest that her lovemaking in this sense has been masturbatory in the most productive of ways: she has been trying to care for herself. And to a degree she succeeds, in that she survives this drama and that she is eventually responsible for liberating both herself and Julio from their roles. Though the process involves her murdering Julio, and hence Sarita's loss of the apparent object of her desire, Fornes hints that Sarita may be on the brink of understanding her desire's misdirection. That even after her various crimes—abandonment of her child, adultery, murder—Mark is at her side at the play's end, providing an audience for her confessions, offers Sarita the opportunity and the context in which she may learn to restructure her desire.

The palimpsests within *The Conduct of Life* are largely formulated by the shifting relationships between Orlando and Nena; his active sexual abuse of her confirms his power over her, but her goodness, her endurance, and her sturdy position over his dead body at the play's end dramatically overturn that narrative.

While Orlando sexualizes every encounter, even comparing the torture of political prisoners to horses mating, the women in the drama undo that imagery. Virtually anticlimactically, Nena's progress is from sexual victim to innocent child, brought up from the torture chamber in the cellar to the safety of the kitchen, where she shells peas with Olimpia. A drama that focuses on the reverberations of political violence characterized by rape and mutilation of genitalia concludes in a space in which circumspect if aggressive women control the stage.

In *Conduct*, as in *Fefu*, Fornes returns to the redemptive possibilities of the relationships between women. Orlando's links with each of the female characters in the play become the models for links between the female characters. The women repeat certain of Orlando's behavior: Leticia sometimes abuses her power over Olimpia; Olimpia mimics Orlando's violent language; Leticia chooses to emulate her husband's denial of his abuse of Nena. But, while all of Orlando's abuses can be characterized as sexual abuses in that they are experienced by his victims as suppression of their human desires, none of the women can indulge in such objectification. Even Leticia, who has jealous cause, can never objectify Nena, as Orlando does everyone who crosses his path, from the political prisoners he tortures to his wife to his abducted child-mistress.

As Nena's literal master, Orlando's abuse of Nena is far more profound than Lloyd and Henry's abuse of Mae in *Mud*. Orlando repeatedly masturbates *against* Nena:

> Look this way [Orlando says to Nena]. I'm going to do something to you. . . . Don't move away. *(As he slides his hand along her side.)* I just want to put my hand here like this. . . . This is all I'm going to do to you. . . . *(He pushes against her and reaches an orgasm.)* (76)

Orlando rapes Nena, makes her his voyeur, his audience, all for the specific sake of overpowering her. Ironically, however, Orlando's corruption of desire obliterates his own self in addition to threatening Nena's. His efforts in the play's final scene to force Leticia into the role of corrupt desirer (he tries to force a "confession" from her concerning a nonexisting lover) results in his erasure from this drama. The sheer violence of his desire can only be destructive.

The brutality of his mastery of Nena prevents any physical escape for her; ominously, her only option is to close off feeling, to lose that part of herself. But, rather than allow that complete repression of herself, Nena desperately pursues her own aptitude for kindness, and she succeeds: "If someone should treat me unkindly, I should not blind myself with rage, but I should see them and receive them, since maybe they are in worse pain than me" (85). Nena transforms her role as Orlando's voyeur into a productive role; she rejects her status as his victim and, in fact, in that manner overpowers him, even while she is physically defeated by him throughout the drama.

Nena's capacity is explicitly dependent on her particular grasp of her role as voyeur, her awareness of the transcendent and complex palimpsests. She understands Orlando's desire for an audience to his sexual behavior because all of her life she has been searching for "anyone watching over me" (84). While Orlando steals his audience—imprisoning his victims, demanding the attention of his spectators—Nena receives her as a gift. Even Nena's monologue explicitly acknowledges the need for an audience, her dependence on her spectators' presence. She tells her story precisely because she believes Olimpia is watching over her, and she concludes her horrible litany of Orlando's abuses with the gift of example: "I should value the things I have. And I should value all those who are near me" (85). In her way Nena is Fornes's most pathetic victim to date— by far the most abused and least able to protect herself from that abuse—and yet

Nena is also Fornes's greatest heroine. Utterly ensnared in a dangerous drama, and in Orlando's violent theatricality, Nena still rejects that role. Nena's image moves from a sexualized object to a spiritual, inviolable agent of good, representing Fornes's theme of the possibility for moral perpetuation by example. By becoming the most powerful figure—the one holding the gun—on *Conduct's* stage, Nena illustrates the transformation of her own palimpsest.

Fornes's most recent published play, *What of the Night?* returns to nearly pure absurdist theater, with particular emphasis on the image as context for the violence of sexuality. The play consists of four plays in turn, *Nadine, Springtime, Lust,* and *Hunger* (some of which have been published and performed independently).[1] While characters may be traced through each play, the context (time and place) differs so completely from play to play that until *Hunger* only characters' names are recognizable. An overall system is suggested by the inclusion of a few familiar elements but undermined by the complete novelty of each new play. That chaotic order is largely what the play is about: it describes the patterns of abuse from adult to child, the consequences of abuse of power, and the explosive fragmentation of the self in a violent world. Each play has at its center a sexually explicit encounter; each encounter is also brief and virtually superimposed on the narrative.

The title character of *Nadine* is an impoverished mother in the Southwest, 1938, a prostitute whose son, Charlie, makes some money for the family by stealing for Pete, who is forty years old, "stupid and mean" (159). Pete is abusive to Charlie; he hits and cheats him and speaks vulgarly to his girlfriend, Birdie. Nadine, in an effort to force Pete to give Charlie more of what he is due, offers Pete sex:

> *Nadine walks behind Pete. She puts her hand inside his jacket and squeezes his breast. He grabs her arm to remove it but begins to shake. His eyes roll. She lowers her hand to his crotch. He quivers. He pants and grunts. His eyes roll.*

Nadine insists, "You got to pay," while Pete *"whimpers and stamps his feet. He growls and drools"* (166). Nadine's seduction resembles abuse; the image of their "successful" sexual encounter (Pete reaches orgasm and gives Nadine three dollars for Charlie, one "on her cleavage" [167]) conveys the violence of these characters' desperation. While *Nadine* ends with the smallest hint of hope when Birdie chooses to leave this stage behind and, in turn, thwarts Pete's efforts to rape her, the image of the only adults on the stage, parental figures of sorts, engaging in something like a mutual rape, suggests that the likelihood of the children escaping unscathed is slight at best.

In *Springtime* even the silhouette of the abusive figure destroys the lives of two lovers. The play centers a male character, whom the audience meets only once, in the midst of a romance between Rainbow and Greta. Midway through the play, and after much talking about him, Ray's brief presence in the women's bedroom is shocking. His intrusion into what is otherwise the women's space destroys the sanctity of that space.

Ray casts a menacing shadow over the women's love affair, imparting danger at his first mention. Rainbow, to earn money for Greta's medicine, has apparently been coerced by Ray into something resembling prostitution: "I had to agree," Rainbow tells Greta, "to do something for him. . . . Meet someone" (84). But Ray's villainy in these women's eyes does not last the course of the drama; either naively or wishfully, the women see his influence over them as redemptive. Though Greta battles both jealousy about Rainbow's relationship with Ray and fear for what Ray does to Rainbow, she also attributes to him the role of a savior. She believes Ray has saved Rainbow from a life of crime, has made her "impeccable" when once she was "peccable" (86). And Rainbow insists that Ray has been a friend to her, that she "understands" him, that "he's not what he appears to be" (85).

From the audience's perspective both Greta and Rainbow are being generous, even ingenuous. The facts appear to be that Ray is Rainbow's pimp and that he hires her out for pornographic photography. He not only takes advantage of Rainbow's need but, eventually, of Greta's need as well. The audience learns that Greta too has been having sex with Ray (or "something," which is all the information Fornes offers), possibly in an effort to free Rainbow from him.

Greta's and Rainbow's romance is never private; it is never only their own but always the man's too. Fornes may be suggesting that a romance between two women can never be their own because the cultural context for romance is heterosexual. Or Fornes may be suggesting that romance in general can never belong solely to its participants, that expectations of the form control the lovers' behavior. Ray controls the progress of Greta and Rainbow's relationship, preventing either of them from ever being truly honest and from giving what they want to give to each other. When Greta discovers Rainbow's photographs, Rainbow says: "I don't mind. It's for you" (87). In order to be able to give her love to Greta, and to take care of her, Rainbow must pass through the conduit of male sexual desire; in order for Greta to save Rainbow's dignity, she too must pass through that conduit. When their relationship ends, the audience is to understand that Rainbow leaves Greta because their relationship does not satisfy her criteria: "For me," she says, "to love is adoring. And to be loved is to be adored" (88). But the audience has no evidence that Greta has not fulfilled her part in Rainbow's formula. The evidence we do have is that Ray has come between them, prevented the women's desire. His sexual role has determined the fate of Greta's and Rainbow's narrative.

Lust opens with Ray, "passionate and driven," and Joseph, "a self-contained businessman," discussing a boy's welfare, Ray urging Joseph to fund the boy's education. While the dialogue runs its formal course ("I'm asking the foundation to help him financially"; "How can I help?" "With a scholarship and additional funds for medical expenses"),

> *Ray speaks, Joseph sits next to him. He reaches for [a] blanket and covers their middle. He puts his arm around Ray's waist and twists him around so Ray's back is to him. He pulls Ray's pants down and begins to move his pelvis against him.* (194)

The visual text of their sexual encounter, which both men admit feels "quite natural" to them, overwrites the literary text. The men's sexual relationship and its power dynamics serve as context for the rest of the relationships in the play.

Helena, Joseph's daughter, enters immediately after the men have zipped up their pants. She is hysterical and needy, almost a parody of what a woman would be in Joseph and Ray's world, and Joseph arranges for Ray to marry her, clearly in order to watch over this ailing woman. The play focuses largely therein on Ray and Helena's inability to communicate and Ray's rise to power over Joseph. A series of Ray's dreams dominate the tableaux, including one in which Ray masturbates against his own image in the mirror while a woman yells angrily at him from another room, and another in which he demands, "Measure my cock" (206), to another unknown woman. Helena ends the play walking her father around the stage until "he becomes more and more debilitated [and] he falls to the ground inert and naked but for his shorts"; she concludes that, though her father knew that if he had a son he could have been "like you [Ray], distasteful in every way . . . he said that he still wished I had been a boy" (218). None of the relationships in this play exist independently of the primary relationship described by the image of the sexual exchange between Joseph and Ray.

A number of characters return for the final play, *Hunger,* compelling the spectator to seek out connections between the other plays, as a rhyme returns the reader to the word it echoes. *Hunger* is an emotionally tender narrative, marked by significantly less violence in the moment but also by the vexing depiction of the characters who have been permanently marred by the violence of the other vignettes from *What of the Night?.* Charlie is now damaged, "a portly old man," "pensive," with "a scar on his forehead" (219). He does not recognize Birdie, his childhood girlfriend, but is drawn to her nonetheless. The sexual encounter in *Hunger* is tentative and tender. Charlie admires Birdie, now seventy-four. He takes her hand, she touches the side of his face, and he puts his arm around her waist and draws her to him: "I would like to know what it feels like to put my body against yours. I knew you'd feel fresh. Like water. Like I've had you in my arms" (225), he says. Though Birdie stops the embrace there, the tenderness of their union—this moment of articulated and imaged desire—pervades the rest of the drama, which offers the portrait of Ray reduced, like King Lear, to homelessness, rage, and fear. The play's final image is the foursome of Birdie, Charlie, Ray, and Ray's companion, Reba; Charlie wraps a blanket around Birdie's shoulder, Reba offers Birdie some sherry to help her ease her way into their world, and Ray, who had harmed Birdie back in *Lust,* "stretches his arm to her," sobbing (235).

An angel enters the abandoned warehouse that houses, and apparently will house forever, these sufferers. The angel too is impaired, "one of his wings is broken and hangs behind him" (219), and he walks, "shuffling his feet with short wide steps" (234). His gracelessness is accentuated by what he has brought to feed the characters; he spills his box full of animal entrails on the floor, and, like animals in turn, the four elderly characters kneel down to eat. Birdie, not yet inured to these victuals, gags and faints. Reba remarks:

> She's not used to this.—*[To the Angel.]* Next time would you bring her something she can eat? Something she likes. *[To Birdie.]* What would you like? . . . Bring her some bread and coffee and some juice and cream. . . . She should have some vegetables, carrot sticks! . . . And also a little red wine. . . . Or sherry's better, I think. . . . Would you like a little liqueur? (235)

Reba is the one character in the final play of *What of the Night?* new to the drama. Her role is defined entirely as caretaker, first of Ray then of Birdie. She has a strength and endurance possible only by having not lived through the first three plays, by coming to life at the moment of her dramatic presence as a nurturer. But, kind as she is, she cannot conceal from the spectator that desire has been reduced to the simple if sensual need for food, as Reba articulates it and as the characters' postures, bent over that food, illustrate.

The repression of characters' desire in *What of the Night?* recalls the repression of *Conduct*'s Nena. Orlando's abuse of Nena in the basement restrains her growth; she remains a child, experiencing desire as a child will for little more than the company and safety available in the kitchen. In Nena, Fornes re-presents all of her victims: victims to others' abuse of power, victims to structures others have created as well as those to which the individual has contributed, to politics and to art. And, in Nena, Fornes re-presents the vulnerability inherent to our theatrical lives. But, in her, Fornes also offers the power of a particular kind of spirit, naive maybe but optimistic enough, young enough, to be entrusted with even the most dangerous of our props and roles—the gun Leticia hands her, the story she asks her to tell.

The goal for perhaps all of Fornes's characters—from the somewhat two-dimensional characters of *Tango Palace* or *The Successful Life of 3* to the complex victimized victimizers of *The Conduct of Life* or *Mud*—is a health that can be characterized sexually, intellectually, and spiritually. To inhabit healthily the theatrical self can mean access to one's sexuality. Many of Fornes's characters seek specifically a sexual contentedness: Leopold, Dr. Kheal, She, Molly, Sarita, Fefu—there is at least one in virtually every play. The process toward that sexual contentedness is self-theatricalization, literally role-playing, performing, soliloquizing, displaying: theatrical seductions of other characters and members of the audience. In turn, a healthy sexuality—self love, in the final account—enables characters to find good roles to play, to rearrange their stages, to rewrite their dramas. Often these moments are the implied moments just beyond the play's end. This could be Nena's fate, Fefu's, Sarita's. And the spectator's.

As may well be said for all theater, the spectator is the final player in Fornes's theater. Sometimes the character of the audience is explicitly acknowledged by Fornes, but, even when that character is less explicit, the audience's role in the creation of the drama is manifest. Spectators play voyeurs in Fornes's drama; their roles as witnesses make them responsible for the turn of events.

The increasingly violent subtexts of Fornes's plays reflect not only the reality of our increasingly violent world but also the more subtle violence to the human spirit that this physical violence does. The transformation of Fornes's characters' sexuality, from She and 3's playfulness, for example, to Orlando's perversities, describes a sensual deadening. In her more recent work many of Fornes's characters die at their drama's end, presumably because by that point in their dramatic and theatrical narratives their bodies are only shells. Fornes's dramas increasingly link sex to violence, not in order to moralize but, rather, to re-present, with impact, the extent of human powers. Fornes's images of the potential violence of role-playing do not strike me as cynical. To the contrary, they are her version of the honest truth meant to spur her audience to action.

Fornes has exceptional respect for, and hence exceptionally high expectations of, her audience; she expects our relationships with her characters to be as honest as are her relationships with them. She expects us to learn from their mistakes. We are to take the theatrical presences of Fornes's characters literally, to locate ourselves within the theatrical presents of her dramas, and then to embrace her theatrical images as wonderfully, or dangerously, real.

Notes

Introduction

1. Toby Silverman Zinman, in "Hen in a Foxhouse: The Absurdist Plays of Maria Irene Fornes" (1990), breaks from the "tradition" of feminist readings of Fornes's plays, citing Fornes's "commitment to the theater, not to politics" (205). Zinman finds *Fefu* to be the paradigm of absurdist theater when and if one seeks out the absurd (her professed task is to illustrate the way "Fornes's drama changes if one changes the lens or the light" [206]). The joke at the center of Fefu's relationship to her husband—and hence, by implication, at the center of women's relationship to men—is, Zinman insists,

> funny and grotesque and horrible all at once, because it is about brutality and self-defeating stupidity, about simultaneous wish fulfillment and wish denial, about the random victim and the victimizer, about the privileging of action over speech and how dangerous that can be; it is about the absurd. (209)

Zinman elaborates her point by exploring in a number of Fornes's plays how the plot, the "different modes of theatrical creation" (210), the emphasis on the image, and the depiction of human desperation makes Fornes an absurdist playwright.

Fornes writes in "I write these messages that come" (1977):

> there is a Mexican joke where there are two Mexicans speaking at a bullfight. One says to the other, "She is pretty, that one over there." The other one says, "Which one?" So the first one takes his rifle and shoots her. He says, "That one, the one that falls."
>
> So in the first draft of the play, Fefu does just that. She takes her rifle and she shoots her husband. He falls. Then she explains that they heard the Mexican joke and she and her husband play that game. That was just my fantasy: thinking of the joke, how absurd it was. (30)

Chapter 1

1. Please see the production and publication history that follows the Notes for other of Fornes's plays, including *Terra Incognita* (1992), which with *What of the Night?* was still being worked on by Fornes at the time of this writing.

Chapter 2

1. I think that Walter Kerr articulates precisely this kind of fearful response, though he couches it in disdain. He writes in the *New York Times* (22 January 1978):

> The seven friends who gather about Fefu . . . unless God in his infinite wisdom strikes them all mute, are very, very philosophical. . . . You may or may not be wondering . . . just how we are able to eavesdrop on a woman who is in bed alone. . . . This is a revolving composition, you understand. . . . Having grown so accustomed to moving about, I did not wait for [the after-production discussion] but kept on going. . . . If I lasted as long as I did, it was because I kept hoping during my constant journeyings that I *might* find a play in the very next room.

I read the subtext of his review as the repulsion he feels about having to overhear so many of women's secrets.

2. In "Multiple Spaces, Simultaneous Action and Illusion" (1987) Stephanie Arnold suggests that by part 3, as a consequence of part 2, the spectators "bring with them a feeling for the characters deepened by the act of entering private spaces and having shared with the characters a suspended moment of time" (263) and that the illusion is heightened by "multiple playing spaces and simultaneous action" (267).

In *Women in American Theater* (1964) Beverly Byers Pevitts writes:

> the audience is experientially involved in the play, not following a linear story. Instead, they overhear conversations, witness a series of encounters. . . . The linkage of the four scenes [in pt. 2] is both linear and vertical. A rhythm of involvement and disengagement works through all six scenes of the play. (317)

3. Fornes told Bonnie Marranca: "I think what makes it special is the fact that there are four walls. . . . the fact that in *Fefu* you are enclosed inside the rooms with the actors is really the difference. . . . Perhaps it's more a question of being a witness . . . " (Marranca 1978, 108).

4. To Bonnie Marranca's question "Do you feel that each of the eight women is symbolic or representative of a female personality type or quality?" Fornes responded:

> I don't think so at all. . . . The fact that *Fefu* is plotless might contribute to the feeling that if the women are not related to each other, and not related to the

plot, then perhaps they represent certain types. In a plot play the woman is either the mother or the sister or the girlfriend or the daughter. The purpose of the character is to serve a plot so the relationship is responding to the needs of the plot. Although *Fefu* is realist, the relationship of the women, in that sense, is abstract. (106)

Lurana Donnels O'Malley offers a different reading of Fornes's work. In her essay "Pressing Clothes/Snapping Beans/Reading Books: Maria Irene Fornes's Women's Work" (1989) she asserts that "several actions involve a kind of liquid nourishment. . . . Although the use of nonnutritional liquids [bourbon] problematizes the model of woman as nurturer, the common element of all these actions [the bringing of liquids] is the sense of self invested in them and the motive of caring and love behind them" (108). O'Malley reads the leaves in the bedroom as symbolic of Fefu inviting "the outside element (leaves, friends, strangers) into her house" (110).

  5. In his essay "*Still playing games:* Ideology and Performance in the Theater of Maria Irene Fornes" (1989) W. B. Worthen theorizes:

> *Fefu and Her Friends* explores the ideology of stage gender through a sophisticated use of stage space to construct a "dramatic" relation between stage and audience. The play conceives the gender dynamics implicit in the realist perspective by disclosing the gendered bias of the spectator's interpretive authority, "his" transcendent position above the women on the stage. (175)

  6. Though Fornes calls the play "realist," Toby Silverman Zinman, in "Hen in a Foxhouse" (1990), warns the spectator and reader against interpreting this play too realistically. She asserts that the final scene

> undoes the tacit realistic explanations of the earlier mysterious story of the deer hunter. . . . The audience's easy, reassuring diagnosis of psychosomatic paralysis is reinforced, especially since we and Fefu see Julia walking in one scene. Look, the spectator can say, see how the male establishment has victimized her and how she has internalized that victimization. This is to assume realism; that is, such a peculiar event must be accounted for, and psychological exegesis is the one most comfortable to our culture. . . . But, if we see the play as absurdist, then the images do not have to be explained; they are theater, not life, and speak with the language of the contemporary stage. (209–10)

For Zinman "Fefu's shooting of the rabbit/Julia is Fornes's rejection of the confining conventions of symbolic realism" (213). Zinman's ultimate purpose seems to be to suggest that what the theater accomplishes is ineffable. Reading Fornes's work as feminist, Zinman asserts, "diminish[es] the play's range and power. Rather than post-Edenic diatribe, Fornes gives us glimpses into the male-female relation in all its dangerous symbiosis. Similarly, she avoids a prefabricated indictment of the failure of devalued language" (218–19). (One might ask why these qualities Zinman finds in Fornes's work precludes that work from being feminist.) Ultimately, Fornes's play satisfies for Zinman the vision of the absurdists:

> absurdist drama is distinguished by its "metaphysical anguish" stemming from our culture's loss of meaning, value, and certitude, as well as by the way such drama communicates this vision through its concrete images, its abandonment of rational discourse, and its insistence on showing rather than saying that life is senseless, thereby revealing a profound mistrust of verbal language. (203–4)

Though I do not accept that Fornes finds the lives of her characters "senseless" (to the contrary), I do share with Zinman a belief that Fornes trusts the image far more than she trusts the word.

7. Though I ultimately disagree with her reading precisely because of what I consider neglect of the image's complexity, in addition to the text's, Helene Keyssar comments, compellingly, that "Fefu kills Julia" in part because she is overwhelmed by "the multiple voices in her head" (1991, 102).

Chapter 3

1. In "Wordscapes of the Body: Performative Language as Gestus in Maria Irene Fornes's Plays" (1990) Deborah R. Geis writes:

> Mae acquires an identity and even a corporeality as she reifies herself through a text. . . . I would suggest that her point of "entry into discourse" [from Jill Dolan's book *The Feminist Spectator as Critic* (1988)] is . . . the act of reading from her textbook. . . . This linguistic recourse allows Mae the power of self-demonstration, the ability to articulate her bodied subjectivity. (300–301)

Geis suggests that Jill Dolan sees Henry as Mae's "entry into discourse," but Dolan never goes so far as to suggest that Mae's movement is successful. Dolan writes, "Unable to learn to read, and now completely objectified by the man who was to grant her entry into discourse, Mae remains outside the register of language" (109).

2. Deborah R. Geis writes:

> Throughout the play, the audience is told that Mae's textbook is "in the center" of the kitchen table. . . . To the extent that Mae refashions herself as a "text," the parallel centricity is evocative, for this moment of *Gestus* embodies Mae's liberation from the representational limits within which she has been confined. (1990, 301)

Lurana Donnels O'Malley offers this reading of *Mud:*

> In *Mud,* Mae is a typical woman/nurturer. She spends three scenes at the ironing board, a symbol of oppression. . . . But in Fornes's work such actions take

on a ritualistic quality which is not completely unappealing. . . . Mae also snaps beans, and packs and unpacks boxes; she is surrounded by two nonbeings. . . . In such a world, the woman is the life force. ("Pressing Clothes" 1989, 106)

3. Alternatively, Bonnie Marranca suggests, "The violence committed in this play is the violence of the inarticulate" (1984, 30).

4. Toby Zinman writes, "The play becomes a photograph album, ironically using the art form most easily associated with realism to break the stage realism" (1990, 217); and Bonnie Marranca writes that the stills "leave room for the audience to enter for contemplative moments. The authorial voice does not demand power over the theatrical experience. . . . There is room for subjectivity, as a corrective to evasive objectification" (1984, 31).

5. Bonnie Marranca writes:

Mud's scenes seem, radically, to be a comment on what does not occur in performance, as if all the action had happened off stage. . . . [Fornes] turns realism upside down by attacking its materialism and in its place emphasizing the interior lives of her characters, not their exterior selves.

Each scene is a strong pictorial unit. Sometimes a scene is only an image, or a few lines of dialogue. This realism is quotational, theatre in close-up, freeze frame. Theatre made by a miniaturist. (1984, 31)

Though I do not think Fornes's method illuminates the "interior lives of her characters," I do think it helps to de-emphasize appearances.

6. Bonnie Marranca offers an alternative reading:

When Henry buys Mae lipstick and a mirror in which to see herself, the moment is not for her a cosmetic action but a recognition of a self in the act of knowing, an objectification, a critique of the self. (1984, 31)

7. Fornes's point here may be partly gender specific. Mae's role is largely determined by her female status, in the context of her responsibilities toward men, in the "female" realm of the kitchen.

Chapter 4

1. See Maida Watson's "The Search for Identity in the Theater of Three Cuban American Female Dramatists" (1991), for a reading of Sarita as Fornes's exploration into Cuban American identity. Watson notes that "the occasional use of Spanish [in Sarita] reflects the bilingual style of the Cuban exile theater." Ultimately, Watson finds that, through Sarita, Fornes "make[s] a statement about the status of Hispanic women" in the United States (193).

2. My descriptions of aspects of spectacle—color, light, set, and so on—are derived from a videotape from the Bill Rose collection at the Lincoln Center Library for Per-

forming Arts, New York City, of the following production: *Sarita,* INTAR; book and lyrics by Fornes; music by Leon Odenz; costumes by Gabriel Berry; lighting by Anne E. Militello; scenery by Donald Eastman, 18 January–19 February 1984, for the Caribbean Currents Festival, with Ballet Hispanico and El Museo Del Barrio.

3. Alternatively, Jill Dolan (1988) makes a distinction between Fornes's treatment of her characters and Richard Foreman's in his production of *Pain(t)*. She suggests that in that work

> Foreman is the extratheatrical protagonist in the narrative of male desire which underlies his work. During [the] performances, he would sit at a console in front of the playing space, running the lights and the sound. By controlling the speed of the taped sound track that often held performers' cues, he was able to manipulate the rate and flow of images, which effected the perceptual difficulty and discomfort he wanted the spectator to undergo. He was the active male who controlled the production and was able to secure his desire. . . . The female body [in *Pain(t)*] is treated as a kind of still life, an object to be arranged and captured like a bowl of fruit or an arrangement of ferns. (53)

Fornes, on the other hand, demonstrates "the Brechtian legacy" for Dolan, by "foregrounding and denaturalizing the representational apparatus" (106).

Dolan summarizes *Sarita:*

> The title character . . . is caught between her conflicting desires for Julio, her violent Latin lover, and Mark, a white man who offers her a ticket out of the oppressions of class and race. Sarita cannot rationally make the leap a liaison with Mark requires, and resorts to killing Julio to free herself from her self-destructive desire. Fornes's theme in [this and other plays] is the hopeless entrapment of women's desire. Her female characters struggle to fulfill themselves sexually or intellectually but are continually, brutally foiled by the controlling male desire and the legal, social superstructure by which it is legitimated. (108)

Chapter 5

1. Deborah R. Geis (1990) suggests that the different nature of the roles that the male and female characters play in this drama is determined by their use of language. She avers that Orlando "uses language to justify a previously defined and circumscribed identity or 'role' rather than creating subjectivity *out* of language" (302).

2. *The Conduct of Life,* written and directed by Maria Irene Fornes, Theater for the New City; set design by T. Owen Baumgartner; costumes by Sally J. Lesser; and lighting by Anne Millitello, March 1985. On videotape in the Billy Rose collection at the Lincoln Center Library for Performing Arts, New York City.

3. Jill Dolan makes a similar assertion, though from a different stance. For an in-depth study of the construction of the spectator and the feminist spectator's place in the theater, see *The Feminist Spectator as Critic* (1988). Dolan claims some of Fornes's work for what she classifies as material feminism. Of *Conduct* she writes, "Fornes illustrates the complicity of women in their mutual oppression, and emphasizes here that gender liberation alone will not serve as an antidote to the inequities of race and class" (108). She adds that texts like Fornes's

> are opened up and completed only in the spectator's reading of them. . . . The spectator is invited to find different meanings through his or her reading of the opened text. Brechtian technique in feminist hands can fragment the realist drama into component parts and expose the gender assumptions for critical inspection. (109–10)

4. Other critics read this last act differently. Stacy Wolf comments that Leticia, in handing Nena the gun, is "pressing the child to take the blame for the crime" (30); W. B. Worthen reads Nena's acceptance of the gun as evidence of her dangerous "Christian humility, an attitude that simply enforces her own objectification, her continued abuse" (174).

Chapter 6

1. An earlier version of *Nadine* was first performed as *The Mothers* at the Padua Hills Festival, Los Angeles, 31 July 1986. *Hunger* was first produced by Engarde Arts, New York City, 1 March 1988. *Springtime* and *Lust* and the four plays as a unit were first performed by the Milwaukee Repertory Theater as *And What of the Night?* 4 March 1989 (*Women on the Verge* 1993, 158).

Appendices

Chronology of Fornes's Productions (Selected)

Tango Palace (originally titled *There! You Died!*)
1963	Actors Workshop, San Francisco
1964	Festival of Two Worlds, Spoleto, Italy
	Actors Studio, New York
1965	Firehouse Theatre, Minneapolis
1968	Tempo Theatre, Boston
	Trinity College, Hartford, Conn.
1973	Theatre Genesis, New York
	U.S. Information Service, Calcutta, India
1974	Academy Theatre, Atlanta
1976	Ohio University, Athens
1978	Rio de Janeiro, Brazil

The Widow
1978	University of Mexico, Mexico, DF (radio)

The Successful Life of 3
1965	Firehouse Theatre, Minneapolis
	The Open Theatre, New York
	Sheridan Square Playhouse, New York
1967	Judson Church, New York
1968	Baird Hall, Chicago
	Little Theatre, London
	Teatro Studio, Caracas, Venezuela
	Kansas State College, Fort Hays, Kans.
	Trinity College, Hartford, Conn.
	Studio Theatre, Amsterdam, The Netherlands
1969	Radio Broadcast, Stockholm, Sweden
	California State College, Fullerton
	Traverse Club, Glasgow, Scotland
	Northeast Missouri State College, Kirkville
1970	The Little Arhus Theatre, Svalegange, Denmark
1971	University of Delaware, Wilmington

Queens College, New York

The Odyssey Theatre, Los Angeles

1972   The Proposition, Cambridge, Mass.

1973   U.S. Information Agency, Calcutta, India

Theatre Intime, Princeton University, Princeton, N.J.

University of California, Irvine

1974   Mullenberg College, Allentown, Pa.

Eastern Iowa Community College

1975   The Orphans, Chicago

The Oxford Players, Oxford

1977   Direct Theatre, New York

Promenade (music by Al Carmine)

1965   Judson Church, New York

1968   California State College, Fullerton

1969   Promenade Theatre, New York

1970   Manhattan College, New York

1971   Pace College, New York

Center Players

Diablo Light Opera Company

Kalamazoo College, Mich.

1972   Kingston Mines, Chicago

1977   Camera Theatre CBS Songs from Promenade

1981   Santa Barbara, Calif.

1984   Theatre Off Park, New York

The Office

1966   Henry Miller Theatre, New York

A Vietnamese Wedding

1967   Washington Square Methodist Church, New York

Moore College, Philadelphia

1968   The Changing Scene, Denver

1969   Yale Cabaret Theatre, New Haven, Conn.

La Mama Experimental Theatre Club, New York

Annunciation

1967   Judson Church, New York

Dr. Kheal

1968   New Dramatists Committee, New York

Village Gate, New York

Judson Church, New York
Berkshire Theatre Festival, Stockbridge, Mass.
Act IV, Provinceton, Mass.
The Changing Scene, Denver
University of Colorado, Boulder
Adelphi College, Garden City, Long Island, N.Y.
Rutgers College, Camden, N.J.
1969 Yale Cabaret Theatre, New Haven, Conn.
Smith College, Northhampton, Mass.
Bucks Country Theatre, N.J.
University of Michigan, Ann Arbor
New Arts Laboratory, London
1970 Community Center, Los Angeles
1971 Dawson Creek, British Columbia
The People Playhouse, New Orleans
Monash Teachers College, Melbourne
1972 U.S. Department of Information Agency, Austria and Germany
University of North Carolina, Chapel Hill
Concord Academy Center, Concord, Mass.
Princeton University, Wilford College
1973 Theatre Genesis, New York
Arkansas College, Little Rock
Wesleyan University, Middleton, Conn.
Grace Episcopal Church, Washington, D.C.
Dickinson College, Carlisle, Pa.
University of Colorado
1974 American Place Theatre, New York
Academy Theatre, Atlanta
George Street Playhouse, New Brunswick, N.J.
1978 Concord Academy, Concord, Mass.
New York Stageworks, New York

The Red Burning Light: or Mission XQ
1968 Open Theatre, Zurich, Milan, and Copenhagen
1969 Cafe LaMama, New York
1974 University Theatre, Urbana, Ill.

Molly's Dream (music by Cosmos Savage)
1968 Boston University—Tanglewood Workshop, Lenox, Mass.
New Dramatists Committee, New York
1973 New York Theatre Strategy, New York
1974 Hartford University, Hartford, Conn.

1975　　　Northern Illinois University, Dekalb, Ill.

The Curse of the Langston House
1972　　　Cincinnati Playhouse in the Park

Aurora (music by John Fitzgibbon)
1972　　　Theatre of the Riverside Church, New York
1974　　　New York Theatre Strategy, New York

Cap-a-Pie (music by Jose Raul Bernardo)
1975　　　INTAR, New York

Fefu and Her Friends
1977　　　New York Theatre Strategy, New York
　　　　　Relativity Media Lab, New York
1978　　　American Place Theatre, New York
　　　　　Wesleyan University, Middleton, Conn.
　　　　　University of Melbourne, Parkville, Australia
1979　　　Victoria College of the Arts, Melbourne
　　　　　Padua Hills Festival, Padua Hills, Calif.
　　　　　Pasadena Playhouse, Pasadena, Calif.
1980　　　Los Angeles Community College, Los Angeles
　　　　　American Musical and Dramatic Academy, New York
1981　　　Eureka Theatre Company, San Francisco
　　　　　The Empty Space, Seattle
　　　　　University of Ottawa
1982　　　Victoria College for the Arts, Melbourne
　　　　　University of Calgary, Alberta
1983　　　Paradise Island Express, Washington, D.C.
　　　　　Theatre Off Park, New York
1984　　　The Blind Parrot Company, Chicago
　　　　　Theatre Aside, Toronto
1985　　　State University College, New Paltz, N.Y.

Lolita in the Garden (music by Richard Weinstock)
1977　　　INTAR, New York

In Service
1978　　　Padua Hills Festival, Padua Hills, Calif.

Eyes on the Harem
1979　　　INTAR, New York

Evelyn Brown (A Diary)
1980   Theatre for the New City, New York

Blood Wedding (adaptation from Federico García Lorca)
1980   INTAR, New York

Life Is Dream (adaptation from Calderon; music by George Quincy)
1981   INTAR, New York

A Visit (music by George Quincy)
1981   Padua Hills Festival, Los Angeles
            Theatre for the New York City, New York

The Danube
1982   Padua Hills Festival, Los Angeles
1983   Theatre for the New City, New York
1984   American Place Theatre, New York
1985   University of Pittsburgh
            Eureka Theatre, San Francisco
1991   Schauspielhaus, Vienna

Mud
1983   Padua Hills Festival, Los Angeles
            Theatre for the New City, New York
1985   Magic Theatre, Omaha, Nebr.
            Theatre for the New City, New York

Sarita (music by Leon Odenz)
1984   INTAR, New York
1985   Eureka Theatre, San Francisco

No Time
1984   Padua Hills Festival, Los Angeles

Abingdon Square
1984   Seattle Repertory Theatre, Seattle (staged reading)
1987   Women's Project and Productions, New York
1989   Theatre Passe Muraille, Toronto
1990   National Theatre, London
            Melbourne Festival, Melbourne
1991   Source Theatre Company, Washington, D.C.

The Conduct of Life
1985   Theatre for the New City, New York

Cold Air (adaptation from Virgilio Pinera)
1985   INTAR, New York

The Trial of Joan of Arc in a Matter of Faith
1986   Theatre for the New City, New York

Art
1986   Theatre for the New City, New York

And What of the Night?
1986   Padua Hills Festival, Los Angeles
1988   En Garde Arts, New York
        Milwaukee Repertory Theatre
1989   Milwaukee Repertory Theatre
1990   Trinity Repertory, Providence, R.I.

Uncle Vanya (adaptation from Chekhov)
1987   Classic Stage Company

Hedda Gabler (adaptation from Ibsen)
1987   Milwaukee Repertory Theatre

Oscar and Bertha
1992   Magic Theatre, San Francisco

Terra Incognita
1991   INTAR and First Amendment, Storm King, New York
1992   Dionysia Theater Festival, Siena, Italy

Chronology of Fornes's Publications

1961   *The Widow,* in *Cuatro Obras de Teatro Cubano* (Havana: Casa de las Americas, Havana, Cuba).
1966   *Tango Palace* and *The Successful Life of 3,* in *Playwrights for Tomorrow* (Minneapolis: University of Minnesota Press).
        Promenade, in *The Bold New Women,* edited by Barbara Alson (Greenwich, Conn.: Fawcett Publications).

The Successful Life of 3, in *Eight Plays from Off Off-Broadway*, edited by Nick Orzel and Michael Smith (New York: Bobbs-Merrill).

1968   *Promenade*, in *The New Underground Theatre*, edited by Robert J. Schroeder (New York: Bantam Books).

   Dr. Kheal, in *Yale Theatre Review* (Yale University, New Haven, Conn.).

1969   *Dr. Kheal*, in *The Best of Off Off-Broadway*, edited by Michael Smith (New York: E. P. Dutton).

1971   *Tango Palace*, in *Concepts of Literature*, compiled by James William Johnson (Englewood Cliffs, N.J.: Prentice-Hall).

   Tango Palace, The Successful Life of 3, Promenade, A Vietnamese Wedding, Molly's Dream, The Red Burning Light, and *Dr. Kheal*, in *Promenade and Other Plays* (New York: Winterhouse Ltd.).

1972   *Molly's Dream*, in *The Off Off-Broadway Book*, edited by Albert Poland and Bruce Mailman (New York: Bobbs-Merrill).

1978   *Fefu and Her Friends*, in *Performing Arts Journal* 2, no. 3.

1979   *Dr. Kheal*, in *A Century of Plays by American Women*, edited by Rachel France (New York: Richards Rosen Press).

   Promenade, in *Great Rock Musicals*, edited by Stanley Richards (New York: Stein and Day).

1980   *Fefu and Her Friends*, in *Word Plays* (New York: Performing Arts Journal Publishers).

1984   *The Danube*, in *Plays from Padua Hills* (New York: Performing Arts Journal Publishers).

   Promenade and Other Plays (New York: Performing Arts Journal Publishers).

1985   *The Danube, Mud, Sarita*, and *The Conduct of Life*, in *Maria Irene Fornes: Plays* (New York: Performing Arts Journal Publishers).

1986   *Lovers and Keepers* (with Tito Puente and Fernando Rivas), in *Plays in Process* (New York: Theatre Communications Group).

   Drowning (adaptation of a story by Chekhov), in *Orchards* (New York: Knopf).

1988   *Abingdon Square*, in *American Theatre* (February) (Theatre Communications Group, N.Y.).

1989   *Abingdon Square*, in *Womenswork* (New York: Applause Theatre Book Publishers).

1991   *Springtime* (from *What of the Night?*), in *Antaeus* (spring 1991)

1993   *What of the Night?* in *Women on the Verge* (New York: Applause Theatre Book Publishers).

Chronology of Fornes's Honors and Awards

1961   John Hay Whitney Foundation fellowship
1962   Centro Mexicano de Escritores fellowship

1965   Obie Award for Distinguished Playwrighting: *Promenade* and *The Successful Life of 3*

1967   Cintas Foundation fellowship
        Yale University fellowship

1968   Yale University fellowship
        Boston University Tanglewood fellowship

1971   Rockefeller Foundation grant

1972   Guggenheim fellowship
        Creative Artist Public Service grant

1974   National Endowment for the Arts grant

1975   Creative Artist Public Service grant

1977   Obie Award for Playwrighting and Directing: *Fefu and Her Friends*

1979   Obie Award for Directing: *Eyes on the Harem*

1982   Obie Award for Outstanding Achievement

1984   Obie Award for Playwrighting and Directing: *The Danube, Sarita,* and *Mud*
        National Endowment for the Arts grant
        Rockefeller Foundation grant

1985   Obie Award for *The Conduct of Life*
        American Academy and Institute of Arts and Letters

1986   Playwrights U.S.A. Award for translation of *Cold Air*

1988   Obie Award for *Abingdon Square*

1990   New York State Governor's Arts Award

Bibliography

Aaron, Jules. 1980, May. Review of *Fefu and Her Friends,* at Greenhouse Theatre, Pasadena, Calif.; written and directed by Maria Irene Fornes; set by Nora Chavooshian. *Theatre Journal* 32, no. 2: 266–67.

Adler, Anthony. 1990, April. "Woman's Work." *Chicago* 39, no. 4: 89–91.

Arnold, Stephanie K. 1987. "Multiple Spaces, Simultaneous Action and Illusion." In *The Theatrical Space,* ed. James Redmond, 259–69. Cambridge: Cambridge University Press.

Austin, Gayle. 1989. "The Madwoman in the Spotlight: Plays of Maria Irene Fornes." *Making a Spectacle: Feminist Essays on Contemporary Women's Theatre,* 76–85. Ann Arbor: University of Michigan Press.

———. 1990. *Feminist Theories for Dramatic Criticism.* Ann Arbor: University of Michigan Press.

Austin, Gayle, and Maria Irene Fornes. 1983. "The 'Woman' Playwright Issue." *Performing Arts Journal* 7, no. 3: 87, 90–91.

Bennet, Susan. 1990. *Theatre Audiences.* London and New York: Routledge.

Bentley, Eric. 1968. *The Theory of the Modern Stage.* Middlesex, Eng.: Penguin Books.

Berman, Paul. 1985, 6 April. Review of *The Conduct of Life. Nation* 240, no. 13: 412–13.

Betsko, Kathleen, and Rachel Koenig. 1987. *Interviews with Contemporary Women Playwrights.* New York: Beech Tree Books/Quill.

Blau, Herbert. 1985. "Odd, Anonymous Needs: The Audience in a Dramatized Society." *Performing Arts Journal* 10, no. 1: 34–42.

———. 1990. *The Audience.* Baltimore and London: Johns Hopkins University Press.

———. 1964, 21 September. Private correspondence to Gerald Freund, associate director of the Rockefeller Foundation; filed at the Lincoln Center Performing Arts Library, New York City.

Brater, Enoch, ed. 1989. *Feminine Focus: The New Women Playwrights.* New York: Oxford University Press.

Brater, Enoch, and Ruby Cohn, eds. 1990. *Around the Absurd.* Ann Arbor: University of Michigan Press.

Carlson, Marvin. 1984. *Theories of the Theatre.* Ithaca and London: Cornell University Press.

Case, Sue-Ellen. 1988. *Feminism and Theater.* New York: Methuen.

———, ed. 1990. *Performing Feminisms: Feminist Critical Theory and Theatre.* Baltimore: Johns Hopkins University Press.

Chekhov, Anton. 1986. "Drowning." *Orchards,* 50–54. New York: Alfred A. Knopf.

Cixous, Hélène. 1984. "Aller à la mer." Trans. Barbara Kerslake. *Modern Drama* 27, no. 4: 546–48.

Cummings, Scott. 1985. "Seeing with Clarity: The Visions of Maria Irene Fornes." *Theater* 17, no. 1: 51–56.

Davy, Kate. 1986. "Constructing the Spectator: Reception, Context, and Address in Lesbian Performance." *Performing Arts Journal* 10, no. 2: 43–52.

de Lauretis, Teresa. 1987. "The Violence of Rhetoric: Considerations of Representation and Gender." In *Technologies of Gender,* ed. T. de Lauretis. Bloomington: Indiana University Press.

Diamond, Elin. 1988, spring. "Brechtian Theory/Feminist Theory: Toward a Gestic Feminist Criticism." *Drama Review* 32, no. 1: 82–94.

———. 1989, March. "Mimesis, Mimicry, and the 'True-Real.'" *Modern Drama* 32, no. 1: 60.

Doane, Mary Ann. 1988–99, Fall–Winter. "Masquerade Reconsidered: Further Thoughts on the Female Spectator." *Discourse: Journal for Theoretical Studies in Media and Culture* 11, no. 1: 42–54.

Dolan, Jill. 1988. *The Feminist Spectator as Critic.* Ann Arbor: UMI Research Press.

Dukore, Bernard F. 1974. *Dramatic Theory and Criticism.* New York: Holt, Rinehart and Winston.

Eco, Umberto. 1977. "Semiotics of Theatrical Performance." *Drama Review* 21, no. 1: 107–17.

Eder, Richard. 1978, 14 January. Review of *Fefu and Her Friends,* at the American Place Theater; written and directed by Maria Irene Fornes; set by Kert Lundell and Nancy Tobias; costumes by Theo Barnes; lighting by Edward M. Greenberg. *New York Times,* 10:1.

Elam, Keir. 1980. *The Semiotics of Theatre and Drama.* London and New York: Methuen.

Esslin, Martin. 1987. *The Field of Drama: How the Signs of Drama Create Meaning on Stage and Screen.* New York: Methuen.

Falk, Florence. 1980, 2 April. "Turning (House)work into Art." *Soho News,* 57, 60.

Feral, Josette. 1984, December. "Writing and Displacement: Women in Theatre." *Modern Drama* 27, no. 4: 549–63.

Fornes, Maria Irene. 1977, December. "I write these messages that come." *Drama Review* 21, no. 4: 25–40.

———. 1983. *Performing Arts Journal* 7, no. 3: 90–99.

———. 1985, September. "Creative Danger." *American Theatre* 2, no. 5: 13, 15.

———. 1987, 12 January. "Notes on Fefu." *Soho Weekly News,* 38.

———. 1994, January. "Special Section: Ages of the Avant Garde." *Performing Arts Journal* 16, no. 1: 21–23.

———. 1978, winter. *Fefu and Her Friends. Performing Arts Journal* 2, no. 3: 112–40.

———. 1986a. *Drowning. Orchards.* New York: Alfred A. Knopf.

———. 1986b. *Maria Irene Fornes: Plays.* Preface by Susan Sontag. New York: PAJ Publications.

———. 1987. *Promenade and Other Plays.* New York: PAJ Publications.

———. 1985, 23 March. Performance of *The Conduct of Life,* at the Theater for the New City, on videotape at the Lincoln Center Library for Performing Arts; written and directed by Maria Irene Fornes.

———. 1984, 16 February. Performance of *Sarita,* at INTAR, on videotape at the Lincoln Center Library for Performing Arts; written and directed by Maria Irene Fornes; music by Leon Odenz.

Francia, Luis H. 1994, 1 March. "Cameos." Review of *It Is It Is Not,* at Theater for the New City; written by Manuel Pereiras Garcia; directed by Maria Irene Fornes. *Village Voice,* 39, no. 9: 84.

Garner, Stanton B., Jr. 1994. *Bodied Spaces: Phenomenology and Performance in Contemporary Drama.* Ithaca and London: Cornell University Press.

Geis, Deborah R. 1990, October. "Wordscapes of the Body: Performative Language as *Gestus* in Maria Irene Fornes's Plays." *Theatre Journal* 42, no. 3: 291–307.

Gussow, Mel. 1986, 17 April. "Stage: 'Lovers' at INTAR." Review of *Lovers and Keepers,* at INTAR; written and directed by Maria Irene Fornes; music by Tito Puente, Fernando Rivas, and Francisco Rodriguez; set by Ricardo Morin; lighting by Anne E. Militello; costumes by Gabriel Berry. *New York Times,* C:25.

Harrington, Stephanie. 1996, 21 April. "Irene Fornes, Playwright: Alice and the Red Queen." *Village Voice* 11, no. 27: 1, 33–34.

Hart, Lynda, ed. 1989. *Making a Spectacle: Feminist Essays on Contemporary Women's Theatre.* Ann Arbor: University of Michigan Press.

Jacobson, Lynn. 1992, April. "Brawl in the Family." *American Theatre* 9, no. 1: 10–11.

Jenkins, Linda Walsh. 1984. "Locating the Language of Gender Experience." *Women and Performance: A Journal of Feminist Theory* 2, no. 1: 5–20.

Kerr, Walter. 1978, 22 January. "Two Plays Swamped by Metaphors." Review of *Fefu and Her Friends,* at the American Place Theater. *New York Times,* 11:3:1.

Keyssar, Helene. 1984. *Feminist Theatre.* New York: Grove Press.

———. 1991, March. "Drama and the Dialogic Imagination: *The Heidi Chronicles* and *Fefu and Her Friends." Modern Drama* 34, no. 1: 88–106.

Kramer, Mimi. 1988, 4 January. "A Brave '*Vanya.*'" Review of *Uncle Vanya,* at the Classic Stage Company; written by Anton Chekhov; directed by Maria Irene Fornes; costumes and set by Gabriel Berry and Donald Eastman. *New Yorker,* 63, no. 46, 59.

Marranca, Bonnie. 1978. "Interview: Maria Irene Fornes." *Performing Arts Journal* 2, no. 3: 106–11.

————. 1984. "The Real Life of Maria Irene Fornes." *Performing Arts Journal* 8, no. 1: 29–34.

————. 1992. "The State of Grace: Maria Irene Fornes at Sixty-Two." *Performing Arts Journal* 14, no. 2: 24–31.

McDonnel, Evelyn. 1992, 2 June. Review of *Oscar and Bertha,* at Magic Theatre; written and directed by Maria Irene Fornes, *Village Voice,* 37, no. 22: 62.

Merrill, Lisa. 1985, 6 June. "Woman of Many Hats Has Just One Vision." *Villager,* 9–10.

Mulvey, Laura. 1975. "Visual Pleasure and Narrative Cinema." *Screen* 16, no. 3: 6–18.

Munk, Erika. 1985, 26 March. Review of *The Conduct of Life,* at Theater for the New City. *Village Voice,* 30, no. 13: 85.

Newton, Edmund. 1975, 5 May. "A Bridge That Doesn't Quite Fill the Gap." Review of Cap-a-Pie, at INTAR; written and directed by Maria Irene Fornes; music by Jose Raul Bernardo. *New York Post, 25.*

O'Malley, Lurana Donnels. 1989. "Pressing Clothes/Snapping Beans/Reading Books: Maria Irene Fornes's Women's Work." *Studies in American Drama, 1945–Present,* 4:103–17.

Paran, Janice. 1987, November. "Redressing Ibsen." *American Theatre* 4, no. 8: 15–20.

————. 1991, October. "Storm King Stopover." *American Theatre* 8, no. 7: 122–23.

Pasolli, Robert. 1969, 17 April. "'You take a yes & a no.'" *Village Voice,* 14, no. 27: 45, 57–60.

Pavis, Patrice. 1982. *Languages of the Stage: Essays in the Semiology of the Theatre.* New York: Performing Arts Journal Publications.

Pevitts, Beverly Byers. 1964. *"Fefu and Her Friends."* In *Women in American Theatre,* ed. Helen Krich Chinoy and Linda Walsh Jenkins, 316–20. New York: Hill and Wang.

Rich, Frank. 1984, 13 March. "Cultural Poisons." Review of *The Danube,* at the American Place Theater; written and directed by Maria Irene Fornes; scenery by Maria Irene Fornes; costumes by Gabriel Berry; lighting by Anne E. Militello; puppets by Estaban Fernandez. *New York Times,* C:3:1.

Schuler, Catherine A. 1986, December. Review of *Maria Irene Fornes: Plays. Theater Journal* 38, no. 4: 514–15.

————. 1990. "Gender Perspective and Violence in the Plays of Maria Irene Fornes and Sam Shepard." In *Modern American Drama: The Female Canon,* ed. June Schlueter, 218–28. Rutherford, N.J.: Fairleigh Dickinson University Press.

Shepard, Richard. 1969, 6 June. "Lyrics Precede Hit Musical's Music." Review of *Promenade,* at the Promenade Theater. *New York Times, 32.*

Shteir, Rachel B. 1991, September. "Women and Authority: Issues Elude Conferees." *American Theatre* 8, no. 6: 53–55.

Smith, Sid. 1988, 8 February. "Chicago rediscovers a theater secret." *Chicago Tribune,* 2:3.

Solomon, Alisa. 1986, 29 July. "Box Variations." Review of *Art,* at INTAR; written by Maria Irene Fornes; directed by Donald Squires. *Village Voice,* 31, no. 30: 81.

Sontag, Susan. 1964. "Against Interpretation." *Against Interpretation*, 3–14. New York: Anchor Books.

Styan, J. L. 1975. *Drama, Stage and Audience*. Cambridge: Cambridge University Press.

Tallmer, Jerry. 1966, 6 August. "Rebellion in the Arts: Toward a New Odets?" *New York Post*, 24.

———. 1987, 15 October. "Let's hear it for Fornes." *New York Post*, 41.

Turner, Victor. 1982. *From Ritual to Theatre*. New York: PAJ Publications.

Waldman, Gloria F. 1985, winter. "Hispanic Theatre in New York." *Journal of Popular Culture* 19, no. 3: 139–47.

Watson, Maida. 1991, May–December. "The Search for Identity in the Theater of Three Cuban American Female Dramatists." *Bilingual Review/Revista Bilingue* (Arizona State University) 16, nos. 2–3: 188–96.

Wetzsteon, Ross. 1977, August. "New York." Review of *Fefu and Her Friends*. *Plays and Players* 24, no. 11: 36–37.

———. 1985, 18 March. "Hidden Treasure." *New York Magazine*, 28.

———. 1986, 19 April. "Irene Fornes: The Elements of Style." *Village Voice*, 31. no. 17: 42–45.

———. 1992, 11 August. "A Different Light: The First Annual Dionysia Festival." *Village Voice*, 37, no. 32: 99–100.

Wilders, John. 1990, 13 April. "A doomed match." Review of *Abingdon Square*, at Cottesloe Theatre. *Times Literary Supplement*, no. 4541: 396.

Willis, Sharon. 1990. "Helene Cixous's *Portrait de Dora:* The Unseen and the Un-scene." *Performing Feminisms: Feminist Critical Theory and Theatre*, 77–91. Baltimore: Johns Hopkins University Press.

Woertendyke, Ruis. 1988, May. Review of *Abingdon Square*. *Theatre Journal* 40, no. 2: 264–66.

Wolf, Stacy. 1992. "Re/presenting Gender, Re/presenting Violence: Feminism, Form and the Plays of Maria Irene Fornes." *Theatre Studies* 37:17–31.

Worthen, W. B. 1989. "*Still playing games:* Ideology and Performance in the Theater of Maria Irene Fornes." In *Feminine Focus*, ed. Enoch Brater, 167–85. New York: Oxford University Press.

Zinman, Toby Silverman. 1990. "Hen in a Foxhouse: The Absurdist Plays of Maria Irene Fornes." In *Around the Absurd: Essays on Modern and Postmodern Drama*, ed. Enoch Brater and Ruby Cohn, 203–20. Ann Arbor: University of Michigan Press.

Index